HEROES
AND
CONTEMPORARIES

Books by David Gower

ANYONE FOR CRICKET?
(with Bob Taylor)

HEROES
AND
CONTEMPORARIES

David Gower

with

Derek Hodgson

COLLINS
8 Grafton Street, London W1
1983

William Collins Sons and Co. Ltd
London · Glasgow · Sydney · Auckland
Toronto · Johannesburg

British Library Cataloguing in Publication Data
Gower, David
Heroes and contemporaries.
1. Cricket players—Biography
I. Title   II. Hodgson, Derek
796.35'8'0922   GV915.A1
ISBN 0 00 217054 X

First published 1983
© David Gower Promotions Ltd 1983

Photoset in Linotron Baskerville by
Rowland Phototypesetting Ltd
Bury St Edmunds, Suffolk
Made and printed in Great Britain by
William Collins Sons and Co. Ltd, Glasgow

CONTENTS

ILLUSTRATIONS

FOREWORD

It seems almost a little late to be writing about heroes. To me, heroes were the people I watched in my schooldays, when the curtains were drawn and the television switched on for the start of a Test match; and the players involved appeared far more mystical than they ever could after my own adoption by the game that I had admired from afar for so long. Sobers was an undoubted hero, as he was no doubt to thousands of other followers – how could anyone with his natural ability and grace not be? Another who easily qualified and who still seems to be playing well in South Africa, was Graeme Pollock, whom I saw score a hundred at Trent Bridge against England in the first Test match my parents ever took me to see. Similarly, John Edrich, when he scored three hundred against the New Zealanders, became another hero.

To me, then, these people, apart from coincidentally all being left-handed batsmen, were extraordinary and worthy of idolization, and that is how they mostly remain. Some of the mystique disappeared when I started to play first-class cricket amongst them; though I shall never play against Sobers or Pollock unless, in the latter's case, the situation in South Africa changes rather quickly. I did just manage to overlap the start of my career with the finish of John Edrich's. My first captain was Ray Illingworth, whose presence when I first reported to Leicestershire overawed me.

What I have gained, therefore, is an understanding of the characters involved, so that the people I have chosen to write about in this book have no lesser ability than my boyhood idols and are thus heroes of the same standing but without the mystique.

Some of them I have played against often; some I have played little against but those have made an impression on me in other ways. It follows that some of these players I do know very well, while with others it has been no more than the odd conversation and casual acquaintance. I can call some of these names close personal friends, while others are virtually strangers.

It would have been easier, I admit, to choose to write only about those I know very well, but that would have meant the omission of several very famous players. I wanted to include players from all over the world who reflect the general standard of the game today. In doing so I apologize to those many players, friends of mine and others, who no doubt feel that they have done enough to merit a mention.

Test status was the qualification for inclusion here in almost every case and the one player who hasn't played Test cricket among my Heroes and Contemporaries has been prevented from doing so only by politics. He has long had the ability to play Test cricket and he certainly qualifies as a hero.

I have tried to make this book about men rather than about cricketers. Fascinating as the game's statistics can be and an endless source of trivia for quizmasters and the like, they are far from being the best judgement on a player and give no insight into a man's character or circumstances. Only, for instance, in the last few years, as biographers have burrowed beneath Edwardian records, have some of the great men of the Golden Age appeared as their contemporaries knew them.

The likes of Boycott and Botham will live forever in the record books, and I am by no means the first observer to try to unravel and explain their complex personalities. I have had the advantage of seeing them in the privacy of the dressing-room, and hope not to have abused that privilege but instead to have used it to good purpose.

Heroes and Contemporaries

The style is, I hope, relaxed and readable. I hope too that the book includes what may be a few new stories about some of your favourite cricketers, and that your enjoyment of them matches the time spent in composing what follows.

Ian Botham

(SOMERSET AND ENGLAND)

Underneath that volcanic public image, Ian Botham is a very genuine sort, as loyal to his friends as he is unforgiving to his enemies. And he's energetically outspoken in both respects! I am glad to count him as a friend, even if it is demanding on one's energy at times.

I had not seen a great deal of him until we met as players for England. He came to Leicester with Somerset in June 1977. He was swinging the ball a lot in those days. I seem to remember that I was not picking up the ball too well – he certainly hit me on the shoulder with a bouncer. I top-edged another over the keeper for 4 – he says I pulled it. I did get some runs (56 and 30) while Botham was bowled by Ken Higgs for a duck. All this was a prelude to our first real meeting in the England dressing room, an experience I shall never forget. Ian has always been boisterous and you always know when he is around. Your one chance of a little peace is if he should take a quick nap – the moment he says 'I'm bored', that's the time to watch out. Your newspaper might suddenly go up in flames, no-one's cricket bag is inviolate; the jokes, the horseplay, the antics will continue until he is obliged to go out to bat, or it is time for lunch.

He is at his brightest and most inventive when things are going well for him, but even in a bad patch he is never down for long. Accidentally or deliberately he was marvellous with Geoff Boycott when he came back into the side, never letting him stay aloof, forcing the general team spirit on him.

13

Rooming with him is enough to give weaker spirits a nervous breakdown. You need a very high tolerance level because Ian's phenomenal energy makes any kind of routine impossible. He cannot go to bed at ten p.m. and wake at eight. I was his room-mate in Sydney for a week in 1978–9 but that worked quite well since it must be said I wasn't too well at the time, having picked up a virus. I spent two or three days in bed and Ian was quiet during that time, so much so that I wondered what was going on. Bernard Thomas has for some reason kept us apart since then and although I did offer to share a room with Ian in Colombo, the lot eventually fell to John Lever.

Once in India, when accommodation was very tight and it seemed that the players and press might have to be mixed up by sharing rooms, the manager, Raman Subba Row and Peter Smith, chairman of the Cricket Writers, drew up a joke list that had Ian sharing with Dick Streeton of *The Times*. Dick, a veteran of the press box, had not endeared himself to Botham with some of his criticisms; also his life-style was quite unlike Ian's. Most though, including Dick, were amused by the apparent pairing until the bluff was called and both were accommodated separately and safely.

Later on that same tour Dick was fiercely critical of Botham's behaviour on the field in Madras; a copy of the paper found its way to the dressing-room. That evening Ian, having had a few lagers after a particularly enervating day in the field, decided he wanted to debate the matter further and stormed up to Dick's room. Accounts of what happened afterwards are hazy from both sides, but it seems that *The Times* man may have out-manoeuvred the world's greatest all-rounder. What isn't disputed is that Dick was most hospitable with his bottle of Johnny Walker and, according to Dick, the pair parted expressing great friendship and mutual esteem. According to Botham, when taxed about the episode the following morning in the dressing-room, a great deal had been discussed and the air cleared. 'What did you say to him?' he was asked. Replied Ian, bringing the house down: 'I can't remember.' Geoff Cook was Ian's original room-mate in India; Ian played him up a lot and nearly wore him out but Geoff, true to style, never complained, although he probably needed a week with Chris Tavaré to recover!

It's impossible to be upset with Ian for long, if only because he's always liable to go off and do something else unpredictable. He can't do anything by halves. He takes his soccer and his golf very seriously; if he drives a car, it's not just to go from A to B or round a circuit. The same with his flying. He has a competitive, killer instinct that makes everything he does a challenge, a drive that is reinforced by colossal reserves of energy. He can do nothing on a small scale. He reduced his golf handicap to eight, starting off a little wayward but, as you can imagine, he hits the ball a very long way. His soccer commitment is a hundred and ten per cent; he once travelled across England for a charity match in Scunthorpe. And when we played a five-a-side match in Guyana, intended as a keep-fit exercise while the political arguments raged, it turned into a fairly serious, not to say dangerous affair.

He's matured as a player, particularly as a batsman in the last couple of years. He never says much when he goes in to bat, rarely much more than 'I'll play as I know how'. What does upset him is to be called a slogger by the press. Ian is openly antagonistic to the media, particularly newspapers, a dislike that dates back mostly to his spell as England's captain. Since then the continuing allegation that he is overweight has angered him and he has never forgiven one newspaper for asking his young son Liam to tell them what his Daddy was eating. When Ian resigned the captaincy, after the first two Tests against Australia in 1981, he implied then that he would never speak to newspapers again. That was the culmination of what must have been the unhappiest spell in his life.

In that previous twelve months he had had back trouble that severely hampered his bowling, making all the difference between slipping two out or perhaps five out, the difference between an important and a mediocre bowling performance.

He led England for nine successive Tests against the world champions West Indies, a job in which no-one could have succeeded a hundred per cent and a job that was undoubtedly a strain on him because inevitably he lost much of the freedom he so enjoys as a player.

As a captain he has many assets: an enormous natural flair for the game, a basic cricket sense, a fund of good ideas of the sort he still offers from slip, a characteristic desire to attack, whether in setting the fields or using bowlers, and a very sound appreciation of all the facets of the game. As he would tell you, he had two great teachers – Brian Close and Mike Brearley. It's true Ian had to learn about leading England as he went along; he didn't always have total support from his players, some of whom did not appreciate his methods of captaincy, but the ranks closed behind him the more the press began to hound him.

He got a duck in each innings at Lord's against the Australians in 1981 and when he walked back through the Long Room I am told it resembled a morgue. Instead of getting behind him then people seemed to turn against him and although there was no lack of sympathy in the dressing-room it was an awkward time for everyone: of the eleven players present there were some confident enough of their own status to offer that sympathy and others who were capable only of letting the situation slide.

It's too easy to say that Ian's return to form was a direct result of his withdrawal from the captaincy. I have to confess, not surprisingly, that there was much gloom in the Leeds dressing-room when the news broke that Monday morning. But then, as the stand between Graham Dilley and Ian developed, our attention grew and so did the crowd's. His knock at Old Trafford was the better of two astonishing innings, being more controlled throughout despite the power of his hitting. Both performances emphasized how much we had lost of him as a player while he was captain. Mike Brearley's return to the captaincy did, however, take the pressure off Ian, resulting in incredible performances with the bat at Leeds and Old Trafford, and with the ball at Edgbaston. Frank Keating relates that the *Guardian* received a reader's letter: 'Sir, on Friday I watched J. M. Brearley directing his fieldsman very carefully. He then looked up at the sun and made a gesture which suggested that it should move a little squarer. Who is this man? Yrs etc.' I'm not really sure that, in fact, Brearley could persuade the sun to move, but he certainly transformed Ian Botham into an Apollo-like figure that summer of 1981.

The Australians learned their lessons, too. Once Ian is under way he can keep going in such devastating fashion that no bowlers can live with him. The mistake they made in England was to try to protect the whole field from him, instead of attempting to restrict him to one side of the wicket. In Australia in 1982–3 he attracted the critics once again, myself included, during his build-up to the Tests, by an apparently over-casual approach to State games. His oft repeated 'Don't worry about me, I'll be all right for the Tests' became increasingly irritating.

When the time came, in the first Test at Perth, the awaited explosion didn't occur. The fortunes didn't smile on him with the bat, and his bowling was generally disappointing. In Adelaide he batted well; he and I thought we might be able to save the match had we been able to last out another session or two. But he was caught at cover, cutting the spinner, a disappointing end from what was perhaps a slight misjudgement. It was a poor shot by the standards of his earlier summers but if two or three more had battled on as bravely as Ian did England would have escaped defeat. In Melbourne the most obvious thing Ian did was to bowl the ball that won the match. Freelance photographer Graham Morris was on his way home to England, flying between Sydney and Singapore. When the news reached him of England's win, he sprayed the plane with champagne shouting 'Botham for God' and was put off at Singapore. That's the effect Ian can have on people!

It was mostly Ian's bowling that worried his friends during the series. He didn't seem to move that potent weapon, his outswinger, tending to bowl only inswing, and he ran in more often like a stock bowler than a strike bowler. In the World Series Cup he had a side-strain which restricted him even further; after Adelaide he admitted he had bowled badly and apologized privately. Bob Willis became loth to put him in to bowl, hesitating to assume that he would bowl ten overs.

For Ian it was a frustrating and mediocre tour and by the end of it he was not in the best physical or mental shape. I believe he needed a break after something like fifty-eight consecutive Tests and fifty-seven consecutive one-day internationals. When the game is going well you feel you can go on playing forever; when you are having a thin time you soon feel exhausted, drained. What Ian needed was time to do the other things he enjoys so much so that he could rekindle his enthusiasm for cricket.

Just before the tour began Ian gave a television interview to Peter Alliss that summed up his philosophy in a way that has rarely been apparent in his other media interviews: 'When the wheel of fortune is stuck with your name on it, you've got to make the most of it, you've got to nail it because there will come a time when nothing goes right. If you could get a hundred, or five wickets, every time you went out you wouldn't be human, you'd just be a machine and there would be no fun in the game. The press built me up into a superstar and then seemed to enjoy hacking away at that statue. The thing I enjoyed most about 1981 was plastering it up again'.

He was then asked about the incident in Madras when Dick Streeton, in common with most of the English press, criticized Botham for making gestures at India's Yashpal Sharma. Ian's reply almost certainly contained what he couldn't remember saying to Streeton! 'It's easy to sit back and criticize from a distance. It's very different out there bowling on a flat slow wicket when it's very hot and the sweat is pouring out of you and you're all keyed up to do well. I've no regrets about what I did.' Peter Alliss then asked Botham what his reaction would be if young Liam had made a similar gesture. Back came that disarming grin: 'I'd probably clip him round the ear.' Ian then explained his attitude as a professional which is something we all share to some degree. 'Cricket may be a game to some but not to me. It's not just a game, it's my living. I give it everything I've got and when I'm doing that I know I am liable to lose my temper.'

That famous temper first won him the attention of the media when he was little more than a boy playing grade cricket in Melbourne. The story goes that Ian Chappell, then at his most famous as Australia's ruthless and winning captain, was supposed to have made some derogatory remarks about England and English cricketers in the hearing of a group inside a bar close by the Melbourne ground, much used by cricketing people. Words were exchanged and the unknown Botham is then supposed to have flared up, dumped Chappell on the seat of his pants and chased him out of the bar. I have heard it said that Ian is still waiting for the chance to finish it off. But, let it be said, I have also seen Ian respond with no more than a smile and a few words to some pretty intense provocation from Australians who were drunk enough to imagine themselves sufficiently tough to take him on.

However his reputation is such that stories, true or false, will always be attributed to him – the press always seems ready to pounce, as with the supposed brawl between Ian and Rodney Hogg in Sydney. It didn't happen. Both sides were invited, on New Year's Eve, to Pier One, a restaurant on a converted wharf in Sydney, to celebrate and watch the fireworks over the harbour. There were seven or eight England players, perhaps four or five Australians. No one stayed till midnight.

Botham, Lamb and myself left about eleven p.m. I was standing with the Australians as my two England colleagues walked past on the way out. There were a couple of jokes and a couple of laughs but certainly no hostility, not even a raised voice – Ian and Rodney Hogg get on well together. When Ian learned what had been published in England his immediate reaction was: 'They're gunning for me again.' When we read something like that abroad, when the player involved is struggling to find some form, the immediate reaction is one of hostility to the press. Once Ian had decided on legal action the affair passed over very quickly and the *Sun* newspaper printed an apology.

Ian found himself in another flare-up over reported remarks about Australian umpires. Doug Insole, the manager, fined him with some reluctance, accepting that Ian believed that any comments he had made were not to be quoted. Later he aroused much sympathy over this in the dressing-room where feelings were running fairly high after the two Sydney Test incidents – when John Dyson's run out wasn't given and when there was the contention over the bat and boot issue with Kim Hughes. Yet in the end Ian had to accept that this time it was his own fault for he knew it was his responsibility to see that anything quoted by him in the newspapers had to be passed by the appropriate authority in advance.

Whatever may be printed to the contrary, Ian Botham is very close to Bob Willis. They have a huge respect for each other's capabilities. Bob has a standard phrase for Ian for when he gets a bit worked up: 'No violence, Guy [this being the original nickname, Guy the Gorilla, bestowed by Geoff Boycott] no violence.' Whatever words may fly between them the basic feeling they have for each other precludes any possibility of a serious rift in friendship or cooperation.

I should emphasize too that the one time Ian played under me I had his complete support. He offered all possible help; you seem to get the best out of him by letting him have his way when setting the field or bowling a spell – then he really does make things happen.

Geoff Boycott

Geoff Boycott is enough of an enigma to puzzle the Sphinx. When he feels wanted, when he knows the proper respect due to him is there, and when he's given a successful and pleasant atmosphere, the old Fireball can glow. Geoff Boycott needs to be happy.

There are at least two sides to Geoff. He must be one of the few people in the world who can make either instant friends or instant enemies.

I never knew Geoff when he was at his peak, indisputably one of the two or three best players in the world. We first met as players when I joined him in the England team shortly after his return from self-imposed exile, in 1978. As a young batsman I was so much aware of his reputation that if he played and missed I was aghast: I didn't expect to see an error from him and anything that passed the bat came as a big surprise.

I shared a third-wicket stand of sixty-one with him in the Second Test against New Zealand at Trent Bridge in August 1978. As I expected, he was very much the senior partner and this was the kind of occasion when he could be so good, talking to you, guiding you, keeping you going. He is so experienced, he has seen it all before and has consequently developed a great sense of anticipation.

Wind and weather, the number of overs bowled, the next fielding change, the next bowling change, how long to the interval, the state of mind of the opposing captain, of the opposing bowlers – all this is going on in Geoff's computer brain while he is playing the very next ball strictly on its merits. Oh, and keeping an eye on his partner, too.

Once he is set into an innings nothing intrudes upon his concentration on the task of building a big one. If he senses that his partner is becoming restless, perhaps itching to have a whack, he will warn about taking risks; but he knows he cannot bat alone, though he likes some partners more than others. He doesn't so much score runs as accumulate them – I think it was John Woodcock, in *The Times*, who named him The Great Accumulator. Geoff has the ability to wait, never becoming distracted, never wavering in his belief that if you stay at the crease the runs will come. At the same time he does harbour secret ambitions to play the cavalier. Those dreams sometimes surface, as when he told me: 'I wish I could play like you, just go out there and cream it around.'

In Barbados once, I was sitting by an hotel pool sampling a pina colada, a sweet, sticky and potent rum-based drink popular in the Caribbean. Geoff took a sip, as he passed, screwed up his face and then, with that famous lop-sided grin, pronounced judgement: 'No wonder you play like you do. If I drank that bloody stuff I'd play some daft shots too.' I have admitted I wouldn't mind some of his application for my game, but his is the last word: 'If I could add your shots to my brain I would be an incredible player.' The irony of all this steely joking is that Geoff Boycott has got the shots, but has revealed them to a select audience on very few occasions, a topic we'll return to later.

I would love to add his self-control, his self denial and his technique to my game. There have been times when I've played as long an innings as Geoff and there are times, I admit, when I've given away a lot of hard work. My thoughts go back to Barbados and the last Test England played there.

Geoff had been given a torrid time by Michael Holding and wasn't feeling too pleased (0 and 1 in the match) and was even less pleased to see me out playing a casual shot at Viv Richards, after battling it out for 54 in the second innings. But although he

was far from happy himself we were able to talk quite openly about my dismissal and he told me he had noticed the signs of relaxation coming into my play. As soon as the fast bowlers had been rested and Viv had come on to bowl he thought that both Graham Gooch and I had eased up. In fact, in the context of a Test match, it wasn't necessary to think in terms of taking runs off Viv. We were there to try to save the match, so the bowling of Richards had to be treated just as seriously as that of Holding. Both Gooch and I knew in our hearts that if Geoff Boycott had been batting at that time he would have come in to tell us about it at the end of the day. To Geoff a Test match is a Test match no matter who is bowling; a 100 always looks better than 50 and is certainly more valuable to the team. This Boycott attitude has rubbed off on some younger members of the England team, although none of us has been able to maintain his astonishing consistency.

I first toured with him in Australia in 1978–9 when he was going through a bad patch. His mother had died, Yorkshire had taken the captaincy away, he was given little peace by the media and in the circumstances it's not surprising that he snapped a few times. He tried to reply, as always, through his bat, playing doggedly throughout and being shaken out of his depression, very often, by Ian Botham. Ian had decided, very early on, that he wasn't going to take any elderly statesman stuff from the famous Yorkshireman. To Boycott's surprise and then, I suspect, secret delight, Ian pulled his leg mercilessly, regularly addressing him as 'Thatch', in reference to his famous hair transplant. Geoff responded by nicknaming Botham 'Guy the Gorilla', one that has stuck and these two great players struck a merry relationship that served England well through many Tests. Now there isn't a great deal of overt respect between them but, after India, they don't take quite the same casual approach to each other either.

On that 1978–79 tour I had a fourth-wicket partnership of 158 with Geoff at Perth. I scored 102, Geoff 77 in seven and a half hours, but it was he who kept me going through that long day. England had lost 3 wickets for 41 and it was essential that Boycott stay there, as he did. I played a few shots and got to my 100 just before the close. As a young player it was the highlight of my career and I was feeling pretty pleased with myself, but I noticed he showed no signs of self-satisfaction. He wasn't saying to himself 'I've done well, I can switch off now.' He was thinking about the next day.

Boycott's ability to secure one end has been invaluable for both Yorkshire and England. When there is a strokemaker going well at the other end it's a perfect partnership, but if Geoff bats with someone who is going through a sticky patch he tends to stagnate that much more. In those circumstances he will allow the bowlers to dictate to his partner. A batsman on form and well set should try to relieve the pressure by scoring runs, forcing the opposition to think again.

Back in England in 1979, Geoff and I shared 191 against India at Edgbaston. He began doggedly; he and Mike Brearley had done all the hard work – as he was quick to tell me – when I arrived at the crease. After that we had some good-humoured, friendly rivalry on a beautiful pitch against bowling that was fairly amiable, once the young Kapil Dev had rested. I tried to get my 50 before he reached his 100. If he hit a 4 I would try to hit one, or two; I saw this as something of a competition but it can't have done him any harm, as he then began to open up and play a few shots himself.

We were to see him in an even better light on the 1979–80 tour of Australia. He was feeling happier for much of that tour and once again, as an England batsman, you knew you couldn't say you had had a good day unless you finished with more runs than he did. What really jolted him then was to be dropped from the one-day side. This was the first World Series Cup, a triangular one-day contest with Australia and the West Indies, in which every match, especially those under the Sydney lights, seemed as hectic as a Cup Final. Geoff had to be recalled at Melbourne where he played very positively and showed he could slap the ball around. Then, at Sydney, in the next floodlit match, he was brilliant. He scored a devastating 105 off only 124 deliveries and made a fool of anyone who ever suggested he lacked the ability or the shots to score quickly. He may not have been too happy playing that kind of cricket but he did leave a huge Australian crowd gaping and gasping for more. It was such a shame that he played like that only when his place was in danger.

That was on 11 December 1979. A month later all had gone sour again. A violent thunderstorm flooded an unprotected Sydney Ground (the ground staff were celebrating New Year's Eve) and, as several experienced observers predicted: 'Whoever won the toss won the Test.' Greg Chappell won and although Boycott didn't want to play, complaining of a stiff neck, Brearley insisted, saying: 'I don't care if you are slightly unfit, I want you to play, I want you in.' England were 1–0 down in a three-Test series and we needed to be at full strength. It was a dreadful wicket to bat on, Boycott getting 8 and 18, but his attitude was never of the best. It was a time he would like to forget and we with him.

I didn't see much of Geoff in the next home series against West Indies, being dropped from the team after the First Test at Trent Bridge. But the West Indians did pay him the compliment of making him their prime target and we all admired the way he stood up to what must have been the most concentrated fast attack in history. He survived. At the age of forty he played through nine Tests against them, at home and in the Caribbean. Clive Lloyd knew very well that Geoff was always the stumbling block. There was much blocking and much more testing of that well-tried defensive technique: he batted on tremendously in his own style, got a century in Antigua and it was no exaggeration to call him the pillar of the team.

He also seemed to have accepted, philosophically, that his long-standing ambition to become England's captain was unlikely ever to be fulfilled. After he had taken over the reins briefly in Pakistan and New Zealand in 1977–8, when Brearley was injured, he was then overlooked when the question of

Brearley's successor arose, in favour of Ian Botham, Brearley again and then Keith Fletcher. Yet Boycott served under Botham happily enough and again under Brearley during that epic 1981 series against Australia. Any misgivings about his availability for a long and difficult tour of India and Sri Lanka were also put aside where he began by fitting in perfectly and doing his job. There were no clouds on those Indian horizons.

To someone as dedicated to scoring runs as Geoff, it must have meant a great deal to him to pass Sobers's record of aggregate Test runs, becoming the heaviest scorer in Test history. Breaking a record of the greatest cricketer of all time is an achievement anyone would have cherished. So it was all the more sad that he should almost immediately retire to his sick bed after Delhi, leaving himself open to criticism and jibes and initiating the first rumours that he might be going home.

I wasn't in the dressing-room that dramatic afternoon in Calcutta during the Fourth Test when he is alleged to have appeared from that sick bed and invited team-mates to a round of golf. Whether he actually took his clubs or just walked round the course I don't know, but by the evening stories were circulating among the players. Officially he was still unwell, although the various doctors called in seem to have given differing accounts of the virus responsible. What isn't in dispute is that Geoff had appeared for lunch that day at Eden Gardens, quiet but bright; he didn't have to crawl in, despite having been in bed for a week. England had finished batting so that all he had to do was field. But he didn't make any fuss, merely packing his bag and saying that the doctors thought him unfit to field and that it would do him some good to stroll around the golf course.

Cricket's unofficial code of conduct lays down that unless you are injured or genuinely unwell – not just off-colour – then you take your place in the field, through the heat and burden of the day. It was Geoff's apparent flouting of this code, more than anything else, that enraged other members of the team. At that time, in Calcutta, I doubt if a single member of the party was a one hundred per cent fit. We all had complaints about little things, coughs and sneezes, tummy rumbles. Whatever afflicts you in India, Delhi-Belly or otherwise, the normal approach is to keep taking the tablets and keep eating what is available to keep your strength up. The right example had been set by Bob Willis who had been really ill for the first month of the tour; he would sit in the dressing-room, after night upon night of sleep disturbed by stomach aches and bathroom visits, only just able to keep his eyes open. If anyone had the right to pull up the ladder it was Willis. Geoff had made do with the steaks served in the best hotels but was much less happy with the food served up-country. Even though most of us felt the same way, it was a question of having to make do in the circumstances. In short, when Geoff went walking instead of fielding he did not have an especially sympathetic audience.

In fact, he touched off an explosion in the England dressing-room. Botham – who would shortly afterwards go down with a nasty virus infection in Madras, sweat through all one night and still go out to bowl the following morning – was especially furious. The extreme view in the dressing-room was that Boycott should never play for England again. Another opinion was that he should be sent home immediately. A third section disagreed, believing that going home was Geoff's objective and that he should now be made to stay to do his job in India. No-one really knew what was in Geoff's mind at that time, only that he seemed as confused as the rest of us.

Initially the attitude of the tour management committee, Raman Subba Row, Fletcher, Willis and Bernard Thomas, seemed to be that Boycott should stay. No-one was having the time of his life; going home, at that point, could seem to be a privilege and an allowance denied the rest of the party. Why should Geoff Boycott be favoured? The issue seemed settled when we heard that Geoff would definitely be going on to Madras with a view to playing in the Fifth Test. Then, while the main party went off by rail to play East Zone in Jamshedpur, rumours multiplied: Boycott was reported to have said he wanted to go, then he didn't, then he did again.

When the final decision was taken that he could fly home from Calcutta the news was delayed, at his request, until he had actually departed, which left the press, the great majority of whom were stuck up-country in Bengal, buzzing like angry wasps. Yet by the time we arrived in Madras the atmosphere had lightened and improved. A day on the coast, a swim in the sea at Fisherman's Cove, the first holiday of the tour for most of the party, helped to raise spirits as we digested the impact of Geoff's arrival at Heathrow in the middle of a tour.

His early departure set up another train of questions. Did he go home early to help arrange the 'rebel' tour of South Africa that followed in March? I can't believe that there can be any truth in that, although his actions laid the basis for the rumours. Only Geoff can supply the full answers to that whole episode. I can say that the initial approaches for South Africa were made before the tour of India began and that Boycott was a key figure in those approaches. He was always keen to go and that those first invitations came from him or his solicitor, Duncan Mutch, is beyond dispute.

In September 1981 the Indian Government were still pondering whether they should admit Boycott and Geoff Cook after their previous South African connections. Mrs Gandhi is said to have been finally convinced that she could take the political risk of allowing the tour to go ahead by a passage in one of Boycott's books, in which he expressed his opposition to apartheid. While I agree that it is possible to abhor a political system yet compete with their sportsmen (e.g. Russia and Argentina) this episode seems to be an example of double-think sufficient to surprise even George Orwell.

There is no doubt that the financial considerations were tempting. Professional sportsmen will always appear to be over-conscious of their earnings to the general public. But what the public often forget, which the professional athlete is some-times too often aware of, is that he may have less than ten years to make the best of his career. So the South African offers involved many arguments, financial and ethical. Was the offer worth jeopardizing a Test career? Would we be supporting an oppressive régime by playing in South Africa? Were we being hypocritical in even considering these offers while playing in India?

For much of the Indian tour the offers lay dormant while players wrestled with the problems. One agent did arrive by a roundabout route, a middle-man trying to give us a nudge in the required direction. We all had to become devious and secretive for an hour or so in turn while we disappeared to talk it over. Then the whole thing seemed to die. I pulled out and several others felt the same way. Once I was out I heard very little of what was going on. What was clear was that Boycott, up until the time he left Calcutta, was the keenest to carry on and go to South Africa.

After his departure it seemed to me that the great majority of the England players felt as I did and that the whole venture would collapse through lack of support. When I returned to England, to depart again on holiday, I was very surprised to read that the South African tour had started and that the party included Graham Gooch who had left me ninety per cent certain that he wasn't going. Yet even if Geoff Boycott hadn't gone to South Africa I doubt if he would have played for England again, no matter how many runs he scored, such was the strength of the dressing-room feeling after Calcutta. The selectors could have chosen him, of course, but they would have had to accept they would have been putting him into an England team that felt much better without him. The anger was such that no one dare say they felt sorry for him, although I think most of us were sad that he could do this to himself, that a man of his standing and prestige in the game could upset so many of his closest colleagues.

It would have been nice for Geoff to have left us at his best when he was happy, wearing his wry grin, talking to you as a colleague. I would prefer to remember the Geoff Boycott who used to offer me advice freely, and talked quietly and sensibly about all aspects of the modern game. He has contributed a lot to English cricket over a long career – perhaps it could have been more. Whatever controversies surround Geoff Boycott, now or in the future, I shall always be glad to listen when he talks cricket sense.

Mike Brearley

(CAMBRIDGE UNIVERSITY,
MIDDLESEX AND ENGLAND)

Rodney Hogg produced the classic remark on Mike Brearley:
'He's the bloke with the degree in people' – but Hogg wasn't
being entirely benevolent when he said that. What he meant
was that England's most successful captain had a trained and
tested ability to measure and judge his fellow human beings
with sometimes unnerving accuracy. He was never at a loss for
an assessment of the incoming batsman, never short of an idea
to try to confound him. Bowlers always need to know how to get
a batsman out – it's part of their memory file – but for other
batsmen to know how to remove the opposition is always so
much harder and not even Mike himself would claim to be a
bowler.

That was just one facet of his talents as a captain. Add
probably the shrewdest tactical brain that has led England in
my lifetime and a decisiveness in his handling of cricket and
cricketers, and you begin to understand the origins of Mike's
successes as England and Middlesex captain. He analysed each
batsman as he walked to the crease and set the field accordingly. Should his initial strategy appear to need revision there
was little hesitation in ordering an immediate re-setting, with
rarely any loss of efficiency. Naturally one cannot do too much
against a batsman playing well and scoring runs, but as a
player under JMB I always felt confident that the right thing
was being done at the right time and that if Australia were
150–2 then it was probably their fault and not his.

He was certainly not averse to gamesmanship. He would talk about a batsman, from slip, loudly enough for the victim to hear (sometimes effective against the novice but unlikely to disconcert most Test players) and discuss field placings with the bowler as though the batsman was no more a difficulty to be removed than a fly brushed off the nose. A number of people who suffered this kind of treatment were put off Mike and termed him arrogant, but they were hardly likely to be on his level. Come to think of it, not many of us would have been on that level, considering the intelligence quotient that emanates from the Brearley brain.

Yet he's not averse to a little gentle fun on and off the field, although he's never allowed it to interfere with the deadly serious business of captaincy. He took the opportunity of a benefit game to pull my leg at the end of my first year of Test cricket, setting a field of three mid-ons and six gullies, thus filling my two supposed weak spots! Mike was very much the professor on Test match eve. It wasn't just motivational stuff but fairly lengthy discussions on opposition strengths and weaknesses, on tactics, on alternative options.

When Botham took over from him the difference was startling; Ian would soon get bored with talking about it and couldn't really wait for the following morning to go out on the field and do it. That's not a reflection on his leadership but a comment on the I.T. Botham Method and he hasn't done badly by it. Whereas Ian relies on instinct and a great feel for the game, Mike was prepared to apply much more constructive analytical thinking to his approach, probably again, much more than most of us could handle at any one time. On the other hand the public may not have realised that the finely controlled and articulate JMB could lose his cool with the best. He does demand total effort all the time on the field, as any captain would, and he hammered it into the England team that you get nowhere in Test cricket without putting the effort in. While he is mostly a man who is very much in charge of himself, his team and very often the opposition, there are some things that can rile him into some very sharp words. For instance, he would never allow heads to drop during a long stand, never let the alertness fade to that point where you play in hope of a wicket rather than play to earn one. Yet strictures pass very quickly with Mike.

He might find it difficult to admit but his brainpower makes it very difficult for him to endure stupidity. Or idiots. He finds it almost impossible to forgive a casual attitude in the game and if he's watching from the pavilion and something occurs that he considers indicates a looseness in either an individual or in team play, then you will hear about it when you get back. He gave Graham Gooch and myself a deservedly stern dressing-down during the Pakistan Test at Lord's in 1978. I had scored 50 and was feeling at least slightly satisfied in my second Test match, to have a second consecutive 50, though I knew that the shot I had played to get out would have earned severe words from my county captain, Ray Illingworth. Gooch had been smacking away, too. We'd been going at about 4 runs an over, marvellous stuff and a great start. Then I played a sweep at Qasim and was bowled, horrendously. When Graham got his 50 he exploded, too, and forfeited his wicket. We came in to a very fierce lecture from the captain who pointed out, rightly, that we should have stayed to turn those fifties into hundreds and the England score would then have been 500 instead of 364; another good basic cricket lesson learned.

Mike admires and respects those who play the game tightly – it must be his Yorkshire ancestry – and he also loves sheer talent. He couldn't always see eye to eye with Geoff Boycott, but got on tremendously well with Ian Botham. Indeed Mike's handling of Botham is one of the most successful aspects of his captaincy. He is one of the people Ian respects totally for the same reasons as the rest of us, and that is why Mike always got the best out of him, a clear example being those last five Australian wickets at Edgbaston in 1981, to wrap up the match. Ian had thought that he should not be bowling at that stage!

That series concluded Mike's captaincy in the best possible

way, a finale with a thunder of drums from Ian Botham. Taking over with England one down and four to play, and somewhat in the doldrums Mike's reputation would probably not have been endangered unduly had we lost again at Headingley – people might have taken the attitude that not even Brearley could have saved that one. The amazing turn-round to that game was obviously Ian's hundred, but to cement the Test in our favour we needed Bob Willis at his inspired best, controlled by Mike Brearley. In that final situation, with so few runs to play with, it helped greatly to feel that the man setting the field would get it right.

I can't decide between Mike Brearley and Ray Illingworth for the place as my best captain. They were both wise and knowledgeable, shrewd and subtle but very different in their approach, a reflection of their different backgrounds: if Mike was more articulate and Raymond more bombastic, I can only suppose they tailored their delivery to their different audiences. What I do find amusing is that wistful look in some Yorkshiremen's eyes when they point out that had the Brearley family not moved to London it is possible, even likely, that Mike would have been a contemporary in the Yorkshire side of Boycott and John Hampshire, and could have been in a position to succeed Brian Close as captain in 1971.

Greg Chappell

We arrived for our 1982–83 tour of Australia to find the locals
hotly involved in the dispute over who should captain the home
side in the forthcoming five-Test series. This did not dismay us
in the slightest – any division in the opposing camp could only
be to our benefit. So we just let them get on with it, thinking
perhaps that our best chance lay in Kim Hughes keeping the
job, after Australia's arduous tour of Pakistan and bearing in
mind the events on Australia's tour of England in 1981. Rodney
Marsh was also a strong contender, having virtually done the
job for some years from behind the stumps, but his candidacy
ended abruptly with the publication of some typically candid
comments in Australian *Playboy* magazine.

The key figure in the debate had already stood down from the
job on more than one occasion for personal and business
reasons; opinion was strong that not even he should be able to
pick and choose at will, but must be willing to give a firm
commitment to the side and to the job.

Greg made his 1,000 runs for Somerset in 1968, an educa-
tional experience for him in more ways than one. When he first
played at Hove he was greeted by a very nasty bouncer from
John Snow that cracked him on the head and removed him
from the field. It says much for Greg's character that he has
never revealed any trace of that shock in his subsequent playing
of fast bowlers. It also explains why he can watch Lawson or
Thomson ping England batsmen around the ears with total

equanimity. Perhaps it runs in the family. Ted Dexter has quoted brother Ian Chappell as saying: 'At the crease my attitude towards bouncers has been that if I'm playing well enough three bouncers an over should be worth 12 runs to me.'

Nowadays Greg assumes a slightly withdrawn attitude to public and press alike; as with some other public figures this leads to accusations of arrogance. He once summed up his motivation on the cricket field by explaining that what he did out in the middle was far more enjoyable than selling insurance, so he would try to keep his game going as long as those feelings persisted.

If things are not going well for any cricketer, considering the alternatives is not a bad way of rekindling enthusiasms. Both in cricket and in business Greg has demonstrated a certain shrewdness over the years that explains his current comfortable position. The off-field pressures of the captaincy probably caused him to relinquish the leadership for the one-day series, quite prepared for Kim to take over the task of talking to the press at the close of play, not to mention the handling of the team throughout the day. Perhaps Greg will not captain Australia again and if that is so then his record, as captain and player, speaks for itself.

At the end of all the argument it was Greg Chappell who was awarded the captaincy. By coincidence the deposed captain Kim Hughes found himself out of favour in his home state of Western Australia, where he was also sacked from his position as the players' representative to the Board. It wasn't a happy time for Kim although, as the records show, he vindicated himself under Greg and proved his worth with the bat, topping the averages.

Greg had the task of justifying his selection as a captain and a player. He had to work knowing that the press and the public would howl for Kim's recall at the slightest mis-step, never mind a stumble.

At Perth, after a shaky start which included some hurried fending-off of short-pitched balls into empty spaces, and taking

a blow on the head from Ian Botham, Greg grew and grew in confidence. He finished with a commanding century during which he demonstrated most of the many strokes in his armoury, before falling to a brilliant catch at third man by Allan Lamb. He also struck a telling psychological blow against Norman Cowans, who was playing in his first Test, by pulling him three times in succession to the mid-wicket fence. It wasn't until Melbourne, in the Fourth Test, that Norman got his revenge. What was most important for Australia after the Perth Test was that Greg was then firmly re-established, ending, at least temporarily, the dangerous and divisive debate on the leadership.

In Brisbane he led Australia to victory in a game which Bob Willis had high hopes of winning. Our failure, first to restrict Kepler Wessels and then to bat adequately in either innings, meant that we could not set a high enough target for the Australians to chase in the fourth innings; although there were jests at the end that suggested, remembering Australian defeats at Edgbaston and Headingley in 1981, that we had perhaps set them too many.

Chappell's best performance of the series came at Adelaide, where his hundred showed authority from the start. Thanks be that we dismissed him on that first day or he might have made another hundred and plenty on the second. As it turned out the Australians had done enough to win the Test, which meant that Greg needed only one more draw to succeed in his ambition to bring back the Ashes to Australia, despite the defeat in Melbourne. This he duly achieved in Sydney where they presented him with 'Urnie', the down-under version of the Ashes urn. His team for the Tests had grown in strength and character as time passed. By circumstance and injury his strongest attack was achieved in Adelaide, when Rodney Hogg joined Lawson and Thomson to form a three-man strike force, supported by Yardley as the spinner and Chappell himself as a relief.

Hogg had previously been dubious about his chances of recall, but I for one have always had a healthy respect for his abilities as a bowler of genuine pace: to my way of thinking he bowled some of the most testing spells of the Series. Rodney is deceptively sharp off the field, too, for underneath those public 'ockerisms' lies a canny dry wit. Of the other two, Lawson seems almost too quiet and sober to be an Australian fast bowler. This mainly teetotal optometry student did, however, keep on taking wickets, and has developed markedly since his visit to England in 1981. Thomson is the same genial man off the field, casual, relaxed with immense public appeal. Rodney Marsh confirms that Jeff can no longer make the ball rise sharply from just short of a length, something that amazed Colin Cowdrey on their first encounter: on five previous tours of Australia, Colin had never met anything like it. But if something of the old fire has gone, Thomson can still strike the gloves regularly and fully justified his recall after a mediocre tour in Pakistan.

Two of Greg's successes and two of my favourite Australians are Bruce Yardley and Allan Border, both have spent time in England and have come to appreciate some of our ways. Bruce is a lovely character, full of stories and humour, a natural mimic and great entertainment value. His task for Greg was to keep one end tidy and controlled while the pacemen hammered away at the other.

Not until Melbourne did we attack Yardley, successfully, putting pressure on Greg to alter his strategy; yet even then Bruce finished with four wickets. Some of his gully catching was unbelievable, if sometimes fallible, while his batting was an irritant to us on several occasions. Our initial counter to his characteristic slash was to post three well deployed third men and fly slips: this worked well enough in three of Bruce's first four innings against us, but not much after that. As for Allan, the batsman we remembered as dominating the Australian innings in 1981 did not reappear until Melbourne. Greg's insistence that Allan bat at No. 3 did nothing for his confidence after a disastrous series in Pakistan. Allan must have been very close to taking a compulsory break from Test cricket for a while, though I imagine that Chappell's support must have kept him there long enough to re-establish himself.

It took Greg a while to assume the responsibility of batting at No. 3 himself. Back at No. 6 Allan was able to assume once again the role he had conquered in the past, that of controlling the closing stages of an innings and acquiring runs himself. Socially, he has an easy-going nature that allows him to be the victim of incessant leg-pulling from the likes of Botham and Lamb. In Ian's case, this is normally the sign of respect and liking, although the recipient is entitled to wonder whether he's not fending off the attentions of an over-friendly bear. When you have just been thrown into the Swan River for the umpteenth time, still clutching a chicken leg and a can of beer, by now largely diluted with salt water, a certain philosophical outlook comes in handy. Fortunately Allan is blessed with such, and managed to keep Ian at bay for most of the tour.

In this sort of spirit the relations between Greg's team and England remained harmonious. More of the Australians maintained the tradition of joining the opposition in the dressing-room at the end of the day. Perhaps they have had more practice, probably none more so than Rodney Marsh, who always seems to be first in, regardless of what might have been happening over the previous six hours. The Australian tour stands out as the most satisfying and enjoyable of them all. On this occasion Australia deserved their success which, obviously detracted somewhat from our own overall enthusiasm, but I cannot imagine any one of our players who wouldn't look forward to returning to those shores.

Brian Davison

It's sad for England and for the rest of the cricket world that South Africa has been denied the chance to display rich cricketing talent at Test level for the past thirteen years (their last Test match was against Australia in 1970). As Allan Lamb demonstrates, the Springboks have their own inimitable and brash, almost arrogant, style: they play cricket with a panache that is almost unique. Although Lamb and Kepler Wessels are the only products of South Africa to play Test cricket recently, county cricket has at least allowed such as Proctor, Barry Richards, Rice, Kirsten, Le Roux and van der Bijl to prove their skills elsewhere than in their homeland, much to the benefit of our first-class cricket.

These men bring enormous strength to the game, and to personify that strength who better than my Leicester colleague, Brian Davison. Whether he is an international is irrelevant, he's most certainly a contemporary hero, a big, hard, very strong man, a product of his army training and of terrorist encounters in the Rhodesian bush. He hits the ball a long way; he can also mis-hit the ball a long way.

Davison has been our main strength at Leicester for a long time, always at or near the top of our averages, with 1982 his best season as a batsman. Now that he is officially English I have to add that he could have done a great job for England in Australia last winter: he'd had two great seasons with Tasmania, had played all Australia's bowlers, was in great form

43

and would have inspired substantially more confidence than some of the players who were chosen.

He is no longer called upon to bowl, though once he was a useful supporting medium pacer, probably with a quick bowler's ambitions. He is still a magnificent fielder whose arm, though it has lost some of its original power, is widely respected round the country. His hands are safe as any, capable of reliable catching at slip or deep midwicket.

For all his abilities what stands out in Brian is his forthright character. He is a man not to be argued with or crossed. He has a straightforward belief in right and wrong and, quite rightly so, it matters not to him who is doing the arguing: Brian has never been one to bow to authority before a question is rightly resolved. This attitude has cost him the captaincy of both Rhodesia and Leicestershire but it has endeared him to all in Tasmania, where he has led the side to no little effect for two seasons.

Earlier in his career this sense of propriety was not so well honed; anyone describing him as wild might not have been far wrong and might also have placed themselves in some physical danger, if slight. There is a now fondly and wryly remembered incident from Yorkshire in one of Brian's earlier county games. An obnoxious little spectator began barracking him: 'Get back to South Africa. We don't want your kind here' and so on, for some time. Then, when Brian dropped a catch, he yelled: 'Told you that you were no good. Get back to bloody Rhodesia.' That did it. Brian disappeared up into the seventeenth row of terracing, apparently in one leap. Everyone's eyes followed him, overlooking that in his fury he had hurled the ball in towards the stumps, where it cracked Mick Norman on the knee. He let out a great howl and went down in a heap while Brian attempted to make his own special point to the gentleman in the crowd.

The anti-South African element in cricket does occasionally fire even wider of the mark. When Northants took the field at Scarborough in September 1981, on the day Ray Illingworth

had suspended Geoff Boycott for talking to the press, (one of those family rows so relished in the Ridings), they had to thread their way through an angry crowd of Boycott supporters. Trying hard not to smile in order to preserve their appearance of absolute neutrality, Geoff Cook and his men were taken aback when one furious Yorkshireman rounded on a Northants player and told him 'And as for you, you've no bloody right to be here at all! Get back to South Africa.' The player he was ordering out was Tim Lamb, younger son of Lord Rochester. Allan Lamb, no doubt maintaining he had an authentic Kéttering accent, was elsewhere.

Brian Davison no longer talks much about his military involvements in Rhodesia/Zimbabwe. As usual, he preferred to be his own man in order to operate outside anyone's immediate authority; by all accounts and not unsurprisingly, he did it well. By contrast his interests away from cricket are now of a gentler nature and, along with spending more time with his family, he has developed an understanding and appreciation of antiques, furniture, painting or china, along with a healthy interest in the grape and some of its finer products, a subject I enjoy 'discussing' with him.

It seems that all the South Africans we have welcomed into county cricket have entertained us well: Barry Richards's strokes, Mike Proctor's competitiveness, the batting and fielding of Peter Kirsten and the all-round skills of Clive Rice, Paddy Clift and Garth le Roux have all added to the public's enjoyment. Off the field, too, they have managed to bring us all some of the flavour and enjoyment that is one of the best aspects of South Africa. Brian is no exception and because of it, he is widely respected and liked after more than ten years' service to Leicestershire. It has been a privilege to have played my cricket with him.

Sunil Gavaskar

(BOMBAY, SOMERSET AND INDIA)

Sunil is a very shrewd little man. The fact that Kapil Dev would replace him as captain of India if he, Sunil, failed to win a series in Pakistan would have been registered long ago in his expectations and calculations. The assumption that Sunil will be captain of India again before his career is over is also logged away in the compartment marked 'Probables'. In the same compartment is the prediction that, barring injury, he will displace Geoff Boycott as the highest scorer in Test history. Sunil is a great batsman and a highly intelligent and subtle captain.

To the obvious assets and gifts of a good player – defensive technique, balance, moving into position early, powerful shots – he has added a formidable power of concentration and application. He is the one batsman in the world who can challenge Boycott in that field. He must have benefitted from his home pitches and from the fairly obvious reluctance of Indian umpires to give him out: winning an lbw decision against Gavaskar in India is almost the equivalent of winning a Test match.

Against that we must balance his sensational start to Test cricket in West Indies in 1970–71. He missed the First Test in Jamaica but after that his scores read 65, 67 not out, 116, 64 not out, 1 and 117 not out, 124 and 220 – his double century in Port of Spain was made in 505 minutes while suffering from severe toothache. The West Indies' attack in that series included

Sobers, Vanburn Holder and Grayson Shillingford; not perhaps Holding, Roberts and Garner but, as Geoff Boycott will be the first to tell you, Test match runs still have to be made, no matter who the opposition or whatever the state of the pitch. Nor would batsmen of that time regard that West Indies attack in any disparaging fashion. Sobers was a great bowler, Holder has a distinguished record home and overseas and Shillingford was a fair bowler in his era.

By the end of the 1979 tour of England Sunil had the astonishing ratio of twenty centuries in fifty Tests, the only comparable player in the game's history being Bradman. In eleven Tests in 1976 he scored 1,024 runs and then surpassed that two years later by amassing 1,044 in only nine!

Perhaps his greatest innings, and certainly the one best remembered in England, was his 221 at the Oval in 1979, when he batted for more than eight hours to steer India into a situation when, after being set 438 to win in 500 minutes, all four results were possible with three balls left.

At home in Bombay Sunil has a son Rohan (named after Kanhai) and he and his wife have to deal with an average of eighty-five fan letters a day. He played in 1980 for Somerset where he stood out – he didn't smoke, drink or swear, although Ian Botham claims he once heard Sunil exclaim 'Oh, my goodness.'

Sunil hasn't always been successful in England where the pitches are more variable. Our quicker bowlers have tried to aim at Sunil's left side of the chest on the basis that as a small man it could be an area of discomfort for him. The theory has worked to some success but he is good enough, and nimble enough, not to be unduly worried. England then found they were more likely to succeed with a pitched-up delivery to catch him in front of the stumps. He did suffer, though, on his last visit to England in 1982 when he was without a regular opening partner. A personal injury and an erratic middle order were further handicaps to him and to his team, and the English public were largely unable to appreciate how difficult a side

India had been at home the previous winter. By the time he broke a leg, fielding silly point to Ian Botham (and never was a fielding position better named than on that occasion) it must have capped a fairly miserable tour for Sunil.

Watching him in India, during our tour, made me realise how much of a diplomat Gavaskar has become. There was a time when he was regarded as a hothead, a man whose career could be blunted by his refusal to acknowledge the Indian cricketing establishment. Since those days Sunil, very much a 'western' Indian in that he has travelled much and lived abroad, has developed a softer approach that has brought him a great deal of influence with the Board of Control while maintaining his semi-divine status with the enormous Indian cricket public. For so smooth a politician it's perhaps remarkable how close Sunil is to Ian Botham, who was in fact chiefly instrumental in persuading him to spend a season with Somerset. There is, of course, an element of mutual wishful admiration: Sunil's game is calculated and reserved while Ian's is more like that of Kapil Dev, spontaneous and volcanic. Certainly Sunil has a high regard for Kapil Dev, whom he has described as his hero. But even if Sunil might like to play with the freedom of a Botham or Dev (in the Jubilee Test at Bombay in 1980 he virtually began his innings by striking John Lever over long on for six) he has settled for his own controlled method of batting and, looking at his figures, he is perfectly justified, for who can argue with such success?

Sunil is a friendly and hospitable character; his current life-style in Bombay allowed him to entertain Ian, Bob Willis and friends with French wine at his flat while elsewhere arguments about umpiring might have been raging. He himself is highly skilled in the handling of umpires, being not above a little cajoling yet, always respectful of their status and their decisions. For the Indians a friendly disposition seems to be a national trait, exemplified by Viswanath, Kirmani and Shastri, to name but three of a cordial eleven. On or off the field it was always easy to chat and relax with them, and they would always be the first to apologise for crowd disturbances or seemingly rough justice from the umpires. Touring India has many enjoyable and pleasant aspects, the only real drawbacks being some of the living and playing conditions up-country. True, there were one or two of the Indian side who got up Botham's nose especially those who score runs and take wickets despite Ian's repeated assertions that they can't play. Sunil took all this with a quiet smile, at a gentle, easy pace, seemingly impervious to any such outside pressures. I would like him in my team.

Graham Gooch

If you ignore Graham's early Test career, which he is probably quite happy to do himself, then he and I came through our England apprenticeship together, starting in 1978. After that we played virtually in every Test – he missed Perth in 1978 – until I was dropped after the Trent Bridge Test against West Indies in 1980. We have been close colleagues and are still good friends. We've known the same feelings at the same stage of our careers, similar successes and failures and there has always been much mutual respect based, perhaps, on the fact that we began our careers playing in a similar style.

I've mentioned elsewhere the Test against Pakistan at Lord's in 1978 when we both scored half-centuries and then received a fierce lecture from Mike Brearley for not staying there and scoring centuries. Graham and I talked a lot about that afterwards, and while we accepted that we fully deserved the captain's strictures we agreed between ourselves that we had to play in our belief that 'if it's there then hit it'. We both came into the game with a lot of natural strokes, with an unfettered approach to playing them, and I hope that neither of us will entirely lose that ambition to play them. What has happened is that we have both improved over the last five years and Graham, particularly, has developed a concentration, determination and a method that have turned him into a great player.

For such a very good player it took Graham a long time to

score his first Test century. For a while the closest he achieved was that 99 in the 1980 Melbourne Test where he allowed Kim Hughes to run him out. I was batting with him at the time and I remember the incident as a stunning, tingling blow. I could see how upset he was, the disappointment lining his face. When something like that happens there is nothing else to do but try to bury it deep into your mind and concentrate on the next time, the next innings. But being run out for 99 in a Test, when it's palpably your own fault, is really impossible to bury. Everyone you meet says either 'Bad luck' if they are a well-wisher or 'You naffing idiot' if they know you well. It's an incident everyone in cricket, world-wide, seems to know about instantly.

Melbourne would have been in the back of his mind for quite a while but he cracked that 'first-ton' barrier in his next series, at home to West Indies in 1980. At Lord's that year he hammered the West Indies quick bowlers around Lord's in what commentators called one of the best innings seen for many a year. It was a crucial innings for him and for England; it established him as an England certainty, apparently for years to come and also helped him to reveal more of the inner Gooch to the public.

Up to then Graham must have appeared as a rather grim, solemn figure of immense power who was prone to moments of simple error, a Darth Varder who could trip up from time to time. His England place assured and his reputation growing, the crowd were able to see something of the dressing-room Gooch, a very honest man who always gives of his best, and a very funny man, both in wit and in his impersonations. His bowling imitations delighted everyone until an Indian batsman and an English umpire, on different occasions, concluded that they were offensive and complained!

Having batted with similar ambitions he and I discovered that we shared a similar sense of humour, best described as Python-esque. Then we began to share our music: he likes George Benson but I've got him listening to Vivaldi and Tchaikovsky. In turn he introduced me to Alan Parsons and there are a dozen contemporary musicians we admire.

It's a shame, both in cricketing and social terms, that Graham is now missing from the England side. As a player he is certainly the man most missed after the 'rebel' ban. That is said with all due respect to such as John Emburey, Derek Underwood and Geoff Boycott, although many felt that Geoff, in the aftermath of the Calcutta incident, should never play for England again. Graham Gooch was the opener we had inked in after his tour of West Indies. He and I were dropped from the Oval Test against Australia in 1981, although we knew that we would be touring India, and perhaps it was that Oval experience which influenced Graham to go to South Africa. I know Graham would have hated the fuss; I know he would have hated being called a rebel. He went because, having weighed everything up, he must have decided it was the right course. 'There are no guarantees' he would often say when selection was being discussed, and he would never take anything for granted, no matter how often we would tell him he was a certainty for a Test place as far ahead as he cared to look. You have to play well to be picked. You have to be scoring runs and if you haven't got those runs behind you then you cannot always be sure you will be in the side, no matter how great a record or reputation. You can always back yourself to play well but no batsman has a legal right to score runs or, and sometimes this is just as important, to have an unbroken run of good luck.

England miss Graham Gooch. We needed him against India, Pakistan and Australia and in the World Cup. I was both sad and happy to read how he pitched into the South Africans on that 'rebel' tour. The ban on the 'rebels' was inevitable from the TCCB's political and financial standpoint, although I feel that a term of three years was too harsh. Though all of those who accepted the South African offer knew of the possibility of a ban, I know from my own involvement in negotiations that attempts were made to insure against that possibility. Perhaps a two-year ban would have been a fair and reasonable decision.

Three years seemed too long unless the Board wanted it to be seen that they were prepared to take a strong line, with the thought that they could always review the ban later, which they still have scope so to do.

I accept that everyone had to make their own decisions and I'm certainly not intending to moralise on the issue just because I didn't go to South Africa. All I can say, in Graham's case, is that right or wrong I wish he hadn't gone. However, players do get dropped and you can't grieve for them. They disappear from the dressing-room and you're sorry they've gone and you miss them, but the new eleven takes over very quickly and redevelops its own character and characters.

Even after three years I expect Graham to be back in the England team. He will be thirty-two, a yet more experienced batsman and I would still back him as a Test opener. His major difficulty might be in displacing one or more of the new school of candidates that emerged in 1982 – Graeme Fowler, Neil Taylor, Mark Benson or anyone else who takes his chance and establishes himself in that position. Whatever happens to Graham, I hope he finds enough challenges in county cricket. Perhaps the captaincy of Essex might provide that when Keith Fletcher retires: it would help him to keep sharp and capable of proving himself again when the ban is lifted.

Richard Hadlee

(CANTERBURY, NOTTINGHAMSHIRE
AND NEW ZEALAND), WITH THE NEW ZEALANDERS

I can pay Richard Hadlee no greater compliment than to say that at his best he comes close to Dennis Lillee, a genuinely great fast bowler. Richard is always a top-class bowler, of firm control with a whippy action, the execution of which appears so effortless and easy that we wonder why we can't all bowl like that.

In the five years since my first encounter with Richard in the Test series of 1978 his reputation has grown appreciably. During that series he rarely bowled with the aggression that marks his best efforts except, notably, during the final Test at Lord's when we needed only 120 to win. Since then, under Clive Rice's fitness regime at Nottingham, he seems to have become more robust, though his slight frame still leaves him a victim of various nagging injuries, such as the hamstring trouble that kept him out of the finals of the World Series Cup competition in Australia. However, he was a major force and vital factor in Nottinghamshire's championship success of 1981, taking more than a hundred wickets.

Where his game has developed markedly since that 1978 series is with the bat. Whereas Ian Botham could then safely regard Richard as a rabbit, to the extent that he claimed his wicket on three out of six occasions (and ran him out on another), reducing his average to just over five for the series, Richard has since scored a Test century and is now a persistent threat from the lower order of the batting. He takes especially to

57

fast medium and medium seam bowling and is very strong when hitting straight and towards midwicket; his record now allows him to be classed as a true all-rounder. Without him the New Zealand side loses much of its threat, yet Richard's contribution is only part of what has become, under Geoff Howarth, an admirable all-round effort. In teamwork New Zealand, a side of resilience, spirit and never-flagging zest, can match anyone.

An always valuable indication of a team's morale and spirit is their fielding standard: the Kiwis never stop running and support each other as if each and every one of them was playing a trial for the All-Blacks. Their bowlers, be it the world-famous Richard Hadlee or someone playing for New Zealand for the first time, appeared to concentrate solely on the basics of length and line, having obviously learned well the first lesson of one-day cricket – keep it tight and then tighten up – let the opposition make the mistakes.

In this way New Zealand as a team played above their known individual form and all credit to Geoff Howarth for inspiring that. He had a poor time himself but led them very well last winter. For once they had a solid, experienced start from Glenn Turner and John Wright, men who know all about run rates. They were followed by Bruce Edgar and Geoff himself. Geoff is lucky in that he does lead a side that contains far more nice guys than prima donnas. John Wright, for instance, is one of the most genuine and generous men in world cricket. Very serious about his own game, and with more than a few theories about other people's, he could eventually be a Test captian.

With the consistency of Jeremy Coney and the enormous hitting potential of Lance Cairns floating up and down the order, New Zealand compensated fully for what appeared to be a weaker bowling line-up, and qualified most convincingly for the one-day finals against Australia. After one convivial evening at the Singapore Cricket Club, while on tour with Derrick Robins' XI, John revealed another talent: someone found him a guitar and he entertained the party to some gently-sung

ballads. John also loves the horses and usually has a hot line to the heart of the matter.

Another New Zealand player to have made an impact on world cricket is Glenn Turner, whose career has been blighted by some long-standing clashes with the New Zealand authorities. There has never been any dispute about his class as a batsman, which he proved initially with a magical series against West Indies when it seemed he could not stop scoring runs. His mentor has been that excellent coach, Billy Ibadulla – it was Billy who took out a gin and tonic to Glenn as he passed his 100, then 200 and finally 300 in 1982 – when he completed his century of centuries.

Almost more remarkable about Glenn's career has been his development as a batsman, from a man with a completely defensive-minded technique who relied on immense concentration and long spells at the crease, into a free stroke player capable of making 300 in a day. Always using an unorthodox grip, he seems to have been one player who has benefitted positively from the demands of one-day cricket – the imperative to play shots. Furthermore he has developed a control that allows him to place shots into gaps, not just through but over a field, dropping them short of any outer ring. He has not endeared himself to purists in recent years, however, with his tactics against quick bowling, when he has opted for allowing himself room and slashing hard towards the off-side. This is not a method normally associated with top-class players, although men such as Bruce Yardley have used it with success, frustrating England on more than one occasion in this way.

Without actually asking Glenn, it's not easy to be sure of his reasons, though it is fair to argue that 40 or 50 runs acquired in this manner on a lively wicket are likely to be of more use than 20 scored by more orthodox means. Perhaps others might prosper similarly if they had the standing to allow themselves to do it. There are no doubt many conflicting opinions!

Meanwhile Geoff Howarth may not have scored as many runs as Glenn, but he is definitely my favourite Kiwi. He has an abundance of natural ability that makes him, in his casual and elegant fashion, a pleasure to watch. Though Surrey may have been disappointed in his overall performances for them, New Zealand will have no such complaints. Geoff has responded well to the New Zealand captaincy and has welded the side together as demonstrated by their success in the World Series Cup and in their subsequent trouncing of England in New Zealand, even if the absence of Richard Hadlee in the Finals left them with a gap they could not quite fill.

The friendliness of Geoff and his side allowed us to play our games in New Zealand in a marvellous atmosphere despite the hard, underlying edge of competition, and some good individual relationships between the players of both sides survive because of it. The matches pulled in big crowds, Antipodean-style, with the sledging we have come to expect from that part of the world, although it does sound a little more good-natured in Wellington and Auckland than it does in Sydney or Melbourne: the New Zealanders have a way of saying 'Good luck, hope you win' in so generous and hospitable a fashion that you almost believe them.

Ray Illingworth

I enjoyed The Captain. Playing under Illingworth was a marvellous experience, going to school under a stern and humorous headmaster whose own foibles make him that much more of a human being. Above all, this headmaster had standards and only if you constantly observed those standards were you admitted to the inner circle of his confidence: no matter how highly Ray might regard you as a player he would not have you in his team, come hell or high water, unless he was utterly convinced that you could do the job he had allocated to you. The winning of matches, the success of the team was far too important for personal considerations, yet there was never any lack of encouragement once he was convinced that the basic talent was present.

I must have met him for the first time in pre-season training around 1975. As a raw second-teamer I saw such men as Ray Illingworth as so far above me that I hardly expected to be noticed; there was an aura about them, as there should be to the young. Later that year I came into the Leicestershire side for the first time which meant, I soon realized, that Illingworth believed something could be made of me. Here I can make my first direct comparison with playing under Mike Brearley, although the circumstances aren't parallel.

If I say that Ray was so much firmer than Mike it was because he was dealing with a kid coming into county cricket. Mike was dealing with England players and he always accorded them that dignity; as a Test player he expected you to know and to do certain things without having to be told.

Illingworth was very fierce about observing certain principles on and off the field. 'You've got to know your ABCs' was a favourite saying, meaning the basic principles of batting, bowling and fielding. Once these were learned thoroughly then he looked for the flair and talent to flesh out a player. With Illingworth you first did your job according to his instructions. You had to look after yourself in what he considered to be a proper manner, both on and off the field. If you did all that then he loved you; if you didn't he would be down on you. He was never a despot, but he could make his displeasure felt.

As is the way of kids when faced with authority there was always a little tendency to needle him gently, a minor attempt to win points back from him. Having been asked if I had had a haircut, my reply of 'No, it fell out in the night' didn't go down too well. But normally he had the last word (at least in the early days). I once turned up at Nottingham wearing one brown shoe and one black. He loved that, seeing the chance to lay into me: 'Been getting up in the dark again, eh?' At Taunton, after giving us all a going over about sloppy dress, I appeared at breakfast in black tie and dinner jacket, calling out 'Morning, captain' as I strolled past. 'Morning, David', he countered. 'Just come in?' Two-nil to Raymond. Old jeans and T-shirts infuriated him. 'Smart casuals' was his order and many cricket teams now dress in what might be called Illingworth style.

Life is never dull under Raymond; there is always a reaction of his to anticipate or strong comment to listen for. This is one saga. One Sunday, playing Essex at Westcliffe, Kenny Mc-Ewan lofted one straight to me at deep midwicket and the ball slipped out of my hands as easily as it went in. Four or five catches went down that day in a generally dismal fielding display. Ray was far from amused and after a few rockets on the lines of 'This game is about doing things properly' he had us working extra hard in fielding practice all the following week.

The next Sunday, at Leicester, Derbyshire's Ashley Harvey-

Walker, facing Raymond, swung the ball high and handsomely to me in the same position on the boundary. This time I had to judge the catch out of a clear blue sky and the ball went in nicely. In huge relief I wellied it high back into the air. As the ball flew up and up I heard an enormous roar from the direction of the stumps: 'GET THE BUGGER IN. IT'S A NO-BALL.' That was Illingworth, starting to do his nut. (Don't forget it was his bowling that had been hit and his runs that were being thrown away.) So I started dragging it down from the sky and then let fly with a flattish throw as the batsmen finished their second run. The ball whacked into the stumps at the bowler's end and then cannoned off through a gap in the field, so there was then a third run to be made while the ball was retrieved. By this time Illingworth was all but dancing with rage.

In his fury he uprooted a stump and hurled it back into the ground with more force than accuracy, just missing a fielder's foot. I doubt if the Derbyshire pair could have taken another run they were laughing so much, while my Leicestershire colleagues had either keeled over or were having hysterics. I came in at the end of the over endeavouring to look suitably repentant and sheepish, by which time the captain had cooled a little: 'Come on, come on, you're not a bloody show pony. When you've caught it get the bugger in straight away and get on wi't bloody game!' And I got a curt 'Don't do that again' at the end of the match. In hindsight the actions and reactions of all concerned remain pricelessly amusing but the lesson is also remembered.

Like Brearley, Raymond is a shrewd judge of a player's capabilities. It has been said that he is too shrewd with his bowlers, especially of his own bowling. He always liked to have fellow off-spinner Jack Birkenshaw test the waters and he always tried to slip in a maiden over before lunch. Unhappily, one day, Javed Miandad was waiting for him and instead of going in with figures of 1-1-0-0 he read 1-0-14-0.

I don't think Raymond had any intention of playing again when he went back to Yorkshire. He wanted to set himself up and he knew he couldn't lead Leicestershire much longer: he wasn't overpaid there when you think of what he had done for the county and how he had brought us all up. Yorkshire offered him a three-year contract as opposed to a one-year; it was an attractive proposition. But Raymond is a great competitor and would always want to play for that reason alone, firmly believing in his own capabilities. He was once playing for Vanburn Holder on a benefit tour in Barbados, in what were 'friendly' exhibition games, when he laid into Bob Willis and Mike Hendrick. In effect he told them that they weren't prepared to try unless there was £10,000 at stake. I thought he was unfair, knowing that Bob and Mike were always fired by donning England colours, but the argument amply demonstrated Raymond's attitude to any and every game of cricket – one hundred per cent effort. So it wasn't a total surprise to hear that he had started playing again at the age of fifty. Yorkshire should benefit from his control on the field and it is up to their junior players to use his experience to the full.

My early career was dominated by Ray Illingworth and none of the lessons I ever learned from him has been forgotten. He was my mentor in the same way that Brian Close was for Ian Botham. I shall always remember that and when I captain a side now I always think that if I can do the job with half of Raymond's ability and success, then I will not be doing badly.

Imran Khan

Imran is one of the world's most influential and powerful players. A superb fast bowler whose great gift is to be able to swing the old ball alarmingly, he is also a high-class batsman with a solid defence and great hitting power. He is a fine fielder too and now a successful Test captain.

That would be a technical description of Imran's cricket. He's also a very combative character, though appearing to some to be over-cool. That slow, deep voice of his seems to have upset a few people, but when I have come across him I can see the determination and sense that has brought him his recent success. He handles his public self in a way that some of us would do well to emulate and, by all accounts, keeps plenty of time for private relaxation. Perhaps Imran is exactly the captain Pakistan needed. They lost the series in England 2-1, albeit closely, but then returned home to rout both Australia and India. Imran seems to have imposed some order and discipline on what was an unruly side. A determined Pakistan, playing as a team, are a match for anyone these days.

If it is correct that the choice of Imran as captain of the side against England in 1982 was a compromise, he being the one player it was thought could unify a team that had split angrily over the original choice, Javed Miandad, then Imran was an inspired selection.

Imran is a cousin of both Majid and Javed Burki, another example of an extremely talented family. He had a catholic education, including schools in Lahore and RGS Worcester before winning an honours degree at Oxford where he was a blue in three successive years, 1973–5. It was in the Parks that he first signalled his outstanding prowess, hitting Notts for 117 not out and 106, then Northants for 170, all in 1974. He played for Worcestershire from 1971–6 and then helped Sussex to win the Gillette Cup in 1978. His loss to Worcester can be gauged from one performance in his last season; 111 not out and 13 for 99 against Lancashire. Superb fast bowling brought him 12 for 165 in the Third Test in Sydney in 1967 to bring Pakistan their first win on Australian soil.

Driven by the need to lead and to set an example, he had a masterly series against England. With proper support from his batsmen he would have led Pakistan to victory at Edgbaston. He did win at Lord's and had Pakistan gone to Leeds leading 1-0, instead of level, they might easily have taken the series.

Lord's is in some sense my story because it was my first Test as captain, Bob Willis having to drop out through injury, a decision that wasn't taken until the morning of the match. That was the worst part of the experience, the uncertainty of not knowing whether I would be in charge; once the decision had been taken and once the match got under way, I enjoyed it. I also quickly learned that captaining a side in a five-day Test match can be exhausting.

Imran won the toss, always a good start for a fresh captain, although I must record that England didn't go into this without practice: Bob and I had had a training session in which I lost the first toss. 'Here,' said Bob, 'use this coin.' I did, I won, took the coin on the field and promptly lost!

After Mohsin's tremendous double century Imran was able to pile on pressure, culminating in the controversy about the ball. Both Imran and Sarfraz swung the ball more than normally through this match, raising suspicions, even allegations, that some extra substance had been applied. Imran didn't surprise us too much in that he has always had the ability to move the ball. Sarfraz is different; he is mostly a seamer – i.e. he moves the ball off the pitch rather than through the air. When

Sarfraz began to swing the ball consistently a few eyebrows went up, notably Ian Botham's, because he really can swing the ball and he wasn't getting anything like the same effect. Nevertheless, I can understand Imran's anger when England recommended that the ball be examined, for he is a tremendous polisher of the ball. The conclusion was that there was no evidence of any tampering with the surface, yet the effect had been so startling, and damaging, to England that I believe we were justified.

Sarfraz wasn't a force again after Lord's and we soon realized that if we could see off Imran and Qadir we could prosper. Once on top Pakistan were tigers; under pressure themselves they tended to disintegrate. Brilliantly as Imran had bowled previously, when it came to the final desperate bid to bowl us out to win at Leeds I feel he tried to bowl too fast and lost his control, leaving Wasim Bari, behind the stumps, scuttling around trying to save the byes.

Imran was their best batsman, a surprising distinction when you think of their famous names, but he was generally more conscientious, the man most aware of the situation and the most consistent. Majid always looks casual, it's part of his game. Zaheer played well at Lord's for a while but seemed to give it away at Birmingham, where he wasn't too well. Haroun had only one Test while Javed, who played well, still has the knack, which he seems to enjoy, of upsetting people. Mudassar did not score as heavily as he might have done and Mohsin, after playing so well at Lord's, helped us out at Leeds with his wild swing at Bob Willis in his first over in the crucial second innings.

The umpires came under fire throughout the series and Imran made the most of the issue in the press, something with which I cannot agree: although there were a number of contentious decisions they were by no means all against the tourists. Such criticisms should be confined to official channels; if any comments are to be made in the press it should be left to the respective correspondents – and not the players – to make them. Otherwise all that is achieved is an unwarranted and unnecessary hostility over and above the normal hard competition one expects from a Test match.

Memories of that series remain fresh, as they are bound to do. At Lord's one saw the difference between a winning Pakistan side and a losing one. At Edgbaston there was the lack of purpose in their batting as England bowled them out; then at Lord's the glee and confidence with which Mohsin and Javed knocked off the 76 runs required showed the other side of Pakistani play. At that point it seemed that Imran had welded them together for the first time in a long time and despite the defeat at Leeds, their two resounding triumphs in the next six months were further evidence of a Pakistan side playing well as a team.

To Imran, whose own performances have remained crucial to the side's success, must go much of the acclaim. His captaincy is no doubt improving with experience, game by game, and while that situation remains Pakistan have the talent and now the purpose to prove what they have previously only threatened.

Allan Lamb

No one is more conscious of being an England player than Allan Lamb; perhaps a fairly obvious statement, remembering his background, yet one that also helps to explain the man and his methods. I admire him as a player, like him as a man and would always want him in my team.

Like most of the South Africans he is a very determined character and I respect the manner in which he was prepared to abandon his upbringing, fight to win an England place and then be just as determined to hang on to it. I imagine he could have made a lot of money by accepting one or more of the numerous offers made to the top South African players to return home and play against the 'rebel' touring teams.

Allan prepared his way into the England team most effectively with four prolific seasons at Northampton. There are not many counties who have not been taken for a century by A. J. Lamb and certainly Leicester have seen him make plenty of good runs. He has always looked a good player, initially favouring the leg side more than he does now, a not uncommon trait among overseas players. He usually seemed in control of his innings, playing the right shots, and plenty of them, from good positions, so it surprised no one when he was picked to represent England at the first available opportunity.

There is an absurdity to his position that he sees as much as I do. I have no objection to having a South African in the England team, particularly if he has British parents. I'm

73

always prepared to abide by the rules and if those rules permit such a qualification and the player in question is good enough to be picked, then picked he should be. At the same time it seems ridiculous that a player like Graham Gooch, who is very much English and totally committed to England, should not be allowed to play for England because he has played in South Africa. The irony of the situation was re-emphasised on the Australian tour by the sight of Australia's No. 1, South African Kepler Wessels, talking to Allan, England's number four, in Afrikaans! Not that Allan is all that brilliant in Afrikaans. His wife Lindsay speaks it much better.

Allan came into the England side in 1982, against India and under pressure. He had been averaging 60 in county cricket, the media had been heralding his arrival for at least a year, but there was and is opposition in some quarters to the selection of a South African. He could not expect the normal sympathy that the public at large and most cricket lovers extend to a new-comer, whether he is batting for his village club, or for England. Allan had to do well, immediately. Fortunately he was able to do that against India, proving his ability to a wider public, the huge television audience, and also scoring some runs. He was much less fortunate against the sharper seam bowling of Pakistan; his luck seemed to change during that series so that he hardly got a run.

Normally Lamb is the opposite of taciturn, a very open character with a great sense of humour, something sorely needed at Lord's in 1982 during the Pakistan Test.

On the Saturday evening, Allan and Lindsay Lamb, Robin Jackman and his wife, and Vicki, my girl-friend, and I set off to have dinner together at Bistro 57 in St John's Wood High Street. The situation on that Saturday evening was that England needed three runs from the last pair at the wicket, one of whom was Robin, to save the follow on. As the acting captain, (Bob Willis having had to stand down through injury) I had great confidence in Jackman. The rest of the story appeared in *Wisden Cricket Monthly*:

At the time all seemed well and the night passed accordingly, despite Robin's insistence on ordering and eating duck, with all the usual cricketer's superstitions being flouted and joked about quite happily – remember that quiet confidence. Indeed, it was not until late on Sunday morning that we began to realize what we had done and to wonder which evil spirits we might have offended: Jackman lbw Imran o.

'What could one say? Any discussion of the merit of the decision quickly became immaterial as the need to start batting again – and better – had to be the first priority. There must have been better situations to be in for a maiden Test captaincy but the belief was also firmly there that the game could quite happily be saved.

'Fairly soon that belief was severely tested, especially after Derek Randall's early dismissal when the next two entries in the scorebook soon read: Lamb lbw b Mudassar o and Gower c Bari b Mudassar o.

'This was the crucial sector of the match: the failure to save the follow on and the quick loss of three wickets. This left the remaining batsmen too much to do, despite the great efforts of Chris Tavaré and Ian Botham. Amidst the seriousness of the situation it didn't take long for someone in the dressing-room, or one of the three ladies in Q Stand, to realize the full power of the St John's Wood High Street Duck: Jackman, Lamb and Gower, all victims.'

Mind you, Robin did say the duck had been very good.

What we did accept, after that Pakistani series, was that Allan was not a No. 3, a position forced on him, as opening the innings was forced on Tavaré, by the loss of Gooch and Boycott. We knew we would have to re-think batting positions radically before we got to Australia, and the summer of 1982 was a time for experiment. It's not true to suggest that either Derek Randall or I refused to open an innings. Randall may not admit it but his attitude will always be 'Wherever you want me, skip. Don't worry about me.' I quite liked the idea of opening in the Prudential one-day matches against Pakistan, whatever my expression may have been as I went out to bat, and was quite pleased with my performances. Before the side for the recent tour of Australia was decided I was rather hoping that Lamb would bat No. 4 and I would be at No. 5 with Botham at No. 6.

By the time we arrived in Sydney the side had changed, for we then had two specialist openers in the party, Geoff Cook and Graeme Fowler. We weren't expecting to play those two and Chris Tavaré, so a No. 3 was needed and various names entered the discussion. We knew Lamb preferred No. 4 and it was felt unfair to ask Derek Randall to move up again: he's happier at No. 6, in fact he's a bonus there. Ian, it was felt, should be inked in at No. 5. So it came back to Gower. I said I would give it a try, although I felt I would be happier at No. 4, but when I got a hundred in my first knock in my new place that settled the argument for a while and gave all the others a chance to settle in. The decision was certainly the right one for Allan Lamb.

He blossomed into his old self as soon as he began to get runs in Australia, making it all the more obvious that the Allan Lamb we had seen in the second half of the summer of 1982 had been a little subdued and a little worried. A stranger would never have noticed, because even in his less confident moments there would be no real clue that this tough little man, full of bounce, had any real doubts about his own ability to succeed.

There was never any question of his not being accepted into the England dressing-room; he fitted in well from the start, he was popular and after a couple of brilliant innings early on in the Australian tour he was the success that his friends and the selectors hoped he would be. He certainly should have made a century and must have cursed himself for getting out in Melbourne, but he always played with great assurance, the result of his work hard, play hard attitude. He produced several fine innings in the one-day series, two of them outstanding; while his 94 against Australia in Melbourne was magnificent.

Allan came back a wiser player in some ways. He knows now he has to toughen up his attitudes a little; perhaps he found county cricket a little too easy. Now he knows that if he is to get big scores in Tests, and he has the talent and the ability to do so, then he needs to be that much hungrier. There are many more runs to come from Allan Lamb.

Dennis Lillee

(WESTERN AUSTRALIA AND
AUSTRALIA), WITH RODNEY MARSH

Though I have played in only three series or tours against D. K.
Lillee the scorebooks record Gower out to Lillee a fair number
of times. I feel that not all those dismissals have been strictly
orthodox, and that on some occasions I was not really beaten by
him, but there are still enough times for me to have to hold up
my hands and admit defeat.

If Dennis isn't the greatest fast bowler then he must come
very close to being so. For a start he's always had great control,
which means that he can vary his length, his line of attack and
his pace at will, and at his peak he was very fast. He can also
adapt, as in the Melbourne Test in 1980 when on a pitch of
uneven bounce and carrying a shoulder injury, he slowed down
to medium fast, rolled his fingers over the ball and with a
mixture of leg-and-off cutters took six English wickets for 60.
On the last tour of Australia it was clear, even before bone
flakes in his knees forced him to withdraw from the Test series,
that he had lost some pace although none of his control nor his
ability to get the crowd roaring as he ran in to bowl.

At Perth I played him at the top of my form in the first
innings and felt as though I could handle anything he let go.
But in the second innings, despite feeling confident again, it
wasn't long before one seamed in and the umpire's finger
confirmed – Gower, lbw Lillee. Later in the tour, after Dennis
had returned for the one-day internationals, the card read –
Gower, b Lillee. Fancying myself to make runs on a good

79

wicket, I had begun to play some shots against Lillee only for one to swing in past an intended extra cover drive to clip the off stump. The motto is simply 'Never relax – this man can bowl.'

Many of Dennis's attitudes to cricket and life are good and positive, yet you cannot forget the blow-ups, the controversies and the gestures until you talk to him at the end of a day's play; then you can appreciate his better side, away from the macho public image. He's big-hearted and a great competitor, very much the player you want on your side. Apart from his vast bowling resources, he is the kind of player who will keep the team going, capable of performing usefully with the bat at the bottom of the order if trouble looms. A very fierce contender, he is typically Australian in that once the play is over he can relax, forget all antagonisms and if there is a hatchet to be buried, it's buried.

You always have to remember with Dennis that he does have a difficult streak that leads him to behave in the way his public expects. Take the famous aluminium bat episode in Perth in December 1979. Judging by subsequent reports from the Australian dressing-room, the rebellious spark had already been lit before he left for the middle and the confrontation with the umpires that ended with his flinging the bat. The whole incident increased its provocation for Dennis as soon as Mike Brearley's reaction became so animated – it was red rag to the bull. Certainly the whole affair took up much more time than it deserved. Then there was the incident with Javed Miandad, during Pakistan's last tour of Australia, culminating in the famous picture of Javed with bat poised, as if to strike Lillee. As I wasn't there I can't pronounce on rights and wrongs, but from all I've read of what happened I would think my sympathies, and those of most players, would be with Dennis. Javed has a very provocative personality, a player who gives even the most mild-mannered opposition good reason, at some time or another, for loss of temper. In that situation Dennis couldn't bear to let Javed appear to get the better of him.

What shouldn't be forgotten is that through most of his

Dennis Lillee, with Rodney Marsh

career Dennis Lillee has enjoyed a good press – that flowing run, that lovely rhythmic action, the regular exciting crash of wickets as stumps go flying or Marsh celebrates another catch. Any boy wanting to bowl fast should study Lillee's action. Like Michael Holding, he is a joy from the moment he starts his run. Lillee is certainly a legend, with Larwood and Lindwall. Another legend, of a different kind, is that of the great Leeds betting coup. England, you remember, were 500-1 against winning that Third Test against Australia on the fourth day, and Dennis has since admitted that he and Rod Marsh took a tidy sum from the bookies at the end of that sensational match. I can believe it: they come from good gambling stock and odds of 500-1 would be irresistible. I can also believe, knowing both players, that placing that bet wouldn't affect their performance in any way. Lillee and Marsh played flat out and tried their hardest for Australia. Dennis, in fact, nearly won the match for Australia with those 17 runs in the second innings, runs that seemed to be getting Australia much too close to the target as far as those of us in the field were concerned.

I can also tell you that quite a few in the England dressing-room were interested in a bet that day, but by the time everyone realised the position the odds had been hastily revised by the bookmakers. No one can condone betting on your own game: clearly it could lead to all kinds of allegations of corruption. Yet I can't blame the Australians for what surely was a unique occasion and, possible, unique odds, in a cricket match.

Dennis has an unconscious genius for turning minor controversies into major headlines. Remember all the shirt-changing discussions of the 1981 series? Dennis picked up a fever in the cold, wet start to their tour and was advised not to play in a damp shirt. That meant that after every bowling spell he had to go off to change his shirt, which roused a certain antagonism: the implication was that Australia's premier fast bowler was getting the chance of rest and treatment in the dressing-room two or three times a day. Even so, this wasn't a big issue until the press exploded it all over the back pages. I'm told it all began with the pre-Test interview of Kim Hughes, Australia's captain, by the Australian press: his defence of Dennis's shirt-changing was interpreted by Fleet Street as an oblique attack on Mike Brearley.

In fact the captains had agreed on a mutually acceptable attitude and all had been settled amicably between the two dressing-rooms, but an angry Brearley took up the English press on this point and with Willis, Botham and Boycott all steamed up about the media, for one reason or another, it was a very good time, from everyone's point of view, for England, so far behind as to be out of sight, to beat Australia in a Test match.

When we arrived in Australia in 1982 we didn't anticipate that we wouldn't see Dennis in action from after the First Test in Perth until the World Series Cup: at Perth he didn't bowl like a man who thought this was his last Test. He bowled some fair bouncers that were quick enough to keep you on your toes, and I had the feeling all along that the moment I relaxed he would produce a very good delivery.

There was some fuss during the Test match when he kicked at a ball that I had played back to him. An lbw appeal, from the previous ball, had been turned down and I put the next one back gently down the wicket. Dennis kicked it well wide and past me and we had a pleasant enough chat at the end of the over. It wasn't, as you might have thought, the first rumblings of World War III.

Sometimes Dennis seems to be deliberately firing himself into attack against a batsman but there is one England player neither he nor any other Australian bowler needs an incentive or stimulant to bowl against – Derek Randall. Randall draws them naturally, just by being himself. I can't vouch for the story that Randall incensed Rodney Hogg, during the 1978–9 series, by humming, whistling, even singing ('You are my sunshine') while Hogg, all tensed up, was running in to bowl. Many an Australian fast bowler has, while about to start his run, stood, hands on hips, while Randall prepares himself, scratching around the crease, twitching, pulling this and setting that – 'Are you frigging ready, then?' More than once Dennis Lillee has set off to bowl while Derek was still amid his multitude of preparations, then has screeched to a halt half-way and glared. The ensuing ritual doesn't vary much. Derek will start his fidgeting again and Dennis will wait until Derek is apparently settled, and then wait a little longer as if to exaggerate the delay. The reaction of the field is normally one of low-key amusement but it all seems to build up Dennis's resentment against the batsman, any batsman.

A big part of the Lillee Legend – and Dennis would be the first to acknowledge it – has been the tremendous support he has received through his career, both for his State and for Australia, from Rodney Marsh, who continues to do a superb job. Marsh is always fascinating to watch, whether keeping to Lillee or any of the fast bowlers. He'll never be a graceful figure because he's a big man, possessing some of the largest calves and legs you will ever see on a cricket field.

Marsh personifies Australian belligerence and will-to-win. Yet, as I have said, once play is over Rod is always one of the first into our dressing-room for a drink and a chat. I enjoy playing against him as an adversary and for his easy, friendly approach off the field. What isn't generally known is that the years of support he has given Lillee, so magnificently that he seems to be cracking an Australian record in every Test he plays, have cost him much pain, in the wear and tear on his knees. It's not unusual for Rod Marsh to come into the England dressing-room with three-inch packs of ice strapped to one or both knees to ease the swelling. You feel honoured to drink with him.

There was a certain sense of reunion in both camps when the Lillee—Marsh axis was restored for the one-day series last winter. Although Dennis hadn't played in any of the Tests after the first he was never far away, turning up at most matches, appearing on television, seemingly reluctant to leave the scene. When he did bowl against us in the one-day series he wasn't quite as fluent, which is understandable. The golden rule remains: when you're batting with Marshy behind you and Dennis running in, never, never relax.

Clive Lloyd

(GUYANA, LANCASHIRE AND WEST INDIES)

A cricket writer once went in search of someone with a long memory who could describe Gilbert Jessop to him. When he at last found an eyewitness the old man said: 'If you can imagine Clive Lloyd as being small, white and right-handed then you've got Jessop!'

I would prefer not to compare Clive to anyone else, alive or dead. He has a style all his own, instantly recognizable, so that if you see any photograph of him, be it in silhouette or reversed or turned into one of the many drawings that now accompany the advertising of cricket products, you would know immediately that it was Clive. He has a distinctive lope out to the wicket, dragging behind him his enormous bat, with the extra grip that smothers the handle. The message is 'Beware' and the general trend is for the inner ring of fieldsmen to retreat a couple of extra yards in case Clive lets one fly.

Stories of Clive's hitting power are legendary. At Leicester, during a large Lloyd century, Ray Illingworth found Graeme McKenzie reluctant to take the second new ball against Clive on the grounds that it was likely to disappear off the bat even quicker than the old one. He was not wrong. On another occasion Clive found one of the smaller Kent grounds to his liking, the Kent bowling even more so and the ball began leaving the ground at fairly regular intervals. An old lady, living nearby, seeing slates bounce off her roof, complained to the police. A sergeant in a Panda car arrived and, not knowing the cricket ground too well, first called at the press box. 'Hello,

hello, what's going on then?' were his reported opening words. The Kent 12th man, who happened to be visiting the box, looked up, saw the uniform, and reported: 'Glad to see you here, Sergeant. It's that big black man out there. I think you should lock him up before he does any more damage.'

Another mighty bombardment hit Derbyshire, in that famous match interrupted by snow, at Buxton. On the Saturday afternoon Clive faced a Derbyshire attack weakened by illness and injury, and the ball began whistling into the town. Richard Streeton had to phone a tea-time report to the *Sunday Times* and concluded it by saying: 'I'm afraid you will have to take a re-write later on. While I have been giving you this copy Clive Lloyd has hit eight sixes.'

Clive is, of course, more than just a big hitter, as a fine Test record proves. He has been scoring big runs at the highest level against all opposition for many years now and has continued to do so despite serious problems with his knees that required operations. Three or four years ago some thought he was approaching the end of a great career when he demolished the Surrey attack in a semi-final, including two colossal hits into the Old Trafford car park off Intikhab. Then, during England's tour of West Indies in 1981 Clive never failed to reach 50 in the four Test matches played. If ever we seemed to have them in trouble – and in Barbados they were 65 for 4 – Lloyd was there to organize resistance. On that occasion West Indies finished on 265, Clive being exactly 100 and Larry Gomes 58, the only real contributors. Throughout the series Clive, good natured as ever, whether being hit on the head by Graham Dilley or despatching the same bowler through point like a tracer bullet (a favourite riposte to the former event), Clive just went on making runs.

As a captain Clive cannot have been too disappointed that the side at his disposal has often contained the most fearsome pace attack ever let loose on Test cricket. Never before have four genuinely quick bowlers lined up on the same side, whatever the combination has been, of Holding, Roberts, Croft,

Clarke, Garner, Marshall and others. Most of the time all Clive has had to do is wind them up and let them go, with the occasional few overs of off spin from Richards or Gomes to provide relief when necessary or to precipitate the arrival of the second new ball. It's not often they have needed the third new ball in recent years!

Whatever one might say about Clive's tactical skills, and there are those who claim them to be limited, he has been West Indies' most enduring and successful captain, so to carp about his leadership seems almost churlish. The captaincy requires a certain amount of diplomatic skill within the team, for inter-island rivalries still play a part in West Indies' cricket politics. There are always personalities in that part of the world who will need to be subdued, at some stage or other, for the good of the team. Clive seems to have managed that so successfully that he has won tremendous respect from not only his own people and players but from cricketers all over the world.

Although Clive and his famous cousin, Lance Gibbs, come from Guyana their mothers were sisters from Barbados, so that cradle of cricketers came very close to adding two more famous names to its tally. Both youngsters developed through the Demerara Cricket Club of Georgetown. Clive's phenomenal outfielding as a younger man is partly explained by his school-boy's athletic record; he was a champion at the 100, 220, 440, 880 yards and both the jumps!

He has had to wear glasses, or contact lenses for a short spell, ever since, as a twelve-year-old, he tried to mediate in a school fight and was hit in the right eye by a ruler, an early example of both the cares and cost of captaincy. Clive's father died when he was sixteen; Clive then had to provide for his mother and three sisters. The additional responsibility was good for his cricket, he says; he had already reached his club first team a year earlier.

By 1966 Clive was competing to enter a Guyana team that already included Fredericks, Kanhai, Butcher and Solomon. A century against Barbados (Sobers and Griffith) followed by 194 at Sabina Park established him in the Shell Shield, but inter-island politics was perhaps one reason why he wasn't chosen for the following tour of England.

His Test career began in India and Sri Lanka. Clive was so petrified that some accident might make him miss it that he refused to ride a motorcycle lent him by a friend. He was even apprehensive about shaving some days in case his hand should slip and cut his throat! It was on that tour, too, that Clive first learned something of the machinations of selection procedure. Frank Worrell told him how lucky he had been to miss England: a Test debut for a batsman was much easier on India's flatter pitches. The Lloyd career then became well-known: Haslingden in the Lancashire League and on to Old Trafford and Lancashire, although the story might have been different had a Warwickshire offer, worth double that of Lancashire's, reached Clive first.

Relations between England and West Indies on the 1981 tour were always good, helped not a little, it's true, by the close personal friendship between England's then captain, Ian Botham, and Viv Richards and Joel Garner, his Somerset team-mates, though even that didn't protect Ian from getting smacked on the helmet by Joel. Clive, too, contributed greatly to a mostly happy tour. He has not only been a delight to watch but a pleasure to play against and we shall certainly miss him when he eventually retires.

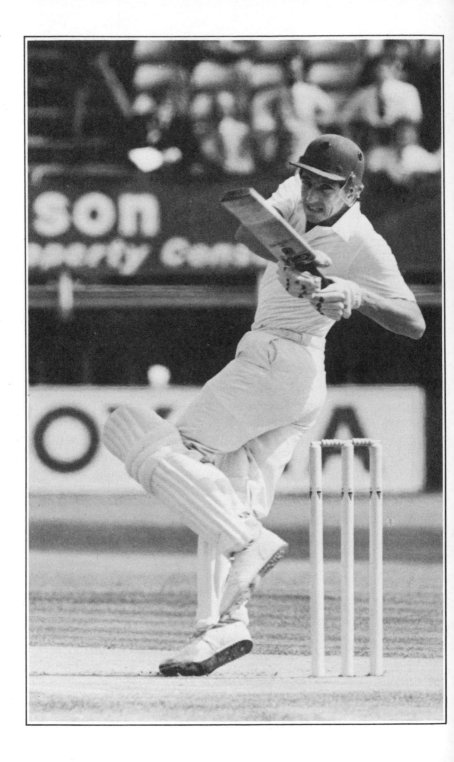

Derek Randall

'Arkle' was his first nickname, the one the public picked up, because he never stopped running. 'Rags' is a little more intimate, probably self-inspired, as if he believes self-denigration will fire him into yet greater performances for Notts and England; it also suits him as a way of describing the loose-fitting appearance his clothes maintain on the field.

His moods can seem to vary with his runs: a couple of good scores under his belt and there's no happier man in the dressing-room; two failures and he tends to withdraw into himself and needs some coaxing to come out again. To some he's the classic clown playing Hamlet, to others the public clown with the private sorrow. Derek Randall has provided world cricket with some great theatre. However, it's not advisable to tell him that to his face. Derek takes his cricket very seriously and has no desire to be tagged forever a 'clown prince' – a television producer who tried to set up an interview before the last Australian tour suggested using that title, and ended up with no interview.

No one tries harder than Randall and no one is prouder of his Notts and England caps and blazers. Everyone takes great pleasure in being Test players, with all the prestige and financial reward that it implies, but honour and glory mean more to some than others; they mean a lot to Derek. Perhaps it's fear of losing that glory that makes him so nervous a character as a batting partner, one you have to watch like a hawk. He was with me when he ran himself out in the last Test against Pakistan at Leeds last year. Watching him as I was, I was still startled when he called for a run and set off. Perhaps I was a little late with my hasty 'no' but there was no run. With Randall, it's up to his partner to be quick enough to stop him suddenly making a suicidal dash. His nerves seem to wind tighter and tighter and the only way he can apparently release the tension is through a burst of energy.

Naturally, this sort of suicide doesn't endear him to many captains or colleagues, but on occasion the comic element can override dour professionalism. It certainly made hilarious television for Channel 9 viewers when he ran himself out against New Zealand in the one-day match in Brisbane, again batting with me. Richie Benaud, commentating on the day's highlights, pointedly drew attention to the expression on our respective faces. Having played one out to deep cover, Derek decided to take two when I was quite happy to settle for one. The first I knew of his decision was the sight of Derek half way back down the wicket, hurtling towards me and the keeper. He didn't stop, even when it was obvious that I was in no position to move, so by the time Warren Lees had lobbed the ball to the bowler's end for the bails to come off, Derek was already thirty yards on his way back to the pavilion. At least we won that game quite comfortably and could look back and enjoy the humour of the incident; in different circumstances it could have been unforgivable.

Derek is a batting enigma. Technically, you couldn't recommend his style; there are times in the dressing-room when we despair while watching him. But he has genius in him and a great eye. He was our most successful batsman against India and Pakistan in 1982 and topped the averages against Australia on tour. His answer to Qadir, Pakistan's superb legspinner, was to mow him over midwicket, googly or not, and his answer to Lawson, Hogg and Thomson was to give them a view of his stumps and drive them hard through cover. His 70 in Sydney mingled luck with genius, so that if he hadn't dragged one on from outside the off-stump, the growing frustration in the Australian attack might have led to a cumulative nervous breakdown. Randall played as only Randall can play.

His other great asset is, of course, his brilliant fielding. His trademarks are the long arms, sleeves buttoned to the wrist, baggy trousers flapping round sprinters' legs; the long stride and high, pumping arms, characteristic of the Randall pursuit; and his habit of starting, as the bowler runs in, from deceptively far back, so that by the time the ball is delivered he is already moving quickly and alarmingly close to the batsman.

Derek's reputation has been made at cover. The first I recollect of this is his running in to throw down the stumps at a Leicester–Notts clash, the batsman well out; many will re-member his run-out of Gordon Greenidge at the start of the 1979 World Cup Final. To add to his speed and accuracy, he has a remarkable pair of hands that have brought him some magnificent catches over the years, including the classic of Andy Roberts in a night match in Sydney and one at cover, in a one-day game against Australia on the last tour, that dismissed Allan Border. It was a brilliant effort, made to look deceptively easy, to keep hold of a very fast-moving ball. Those same hands have brought him into close catching positions, although he has never been too enthusiastic about standing at 'Boot Hill', at forward short leg. He has made great catches and marvellous stops everywhere on the field; but then, he has also been responsible for some truly casual dropped chances and wild overthrows. During the Australian second innings in the Ade-laide Test last winter, one of Derek's rockets brought a wry aside from Chris Tavaré to Eddie Hemmings: 'He's just thrown that ball for more runs than we've made in the whole match.'

Concentration is essential wherever you field, although the priorities are different according to position: at cover you watch the feet and hands to anticipate the shot, while slip is mostly watching the bat, from which the edge will come. Bobby Simpson, for instance, is reckoned to be one of the greatest slips fielders, regarded by many as the best since 1945. Talking to Keith Andrew, himself an England wicketkeeper and national coach, Bob enlarged on this question of concentration: 'I bent down as late as possible. I didn't waste concentration while a fellow was running in to bowl. I'd wait till he was nearly there and then go down, focused, ready, and then up again.'

A change of positions keeps the mind fresh and helps a player keep his application through the day. Tavaré, for instance, although he has been one of the best slips in the country, likes to move into the outfield occasionally. Chris is a good example of what can happen to a Test-class fielder. Confidence is the key, crucial if a slip is to be alert and safe. Having been a most reliable slip for two or three years, he started to lose that confidence. His troubles probably began in India where, after badly bruising his hands at catching practice, he started dropping a disproportionate number of chances, with the result that he asked not to field at slip. Even now he can still remember the nightmare of that period – and I shudder to think the effect on him had not Geoff Miller held the rebound from Chris's hands to win the Melbourne Test by three runs.

Fielding is now so sharp, thanks to one-day cricket, that even an average mistake can bring a groan from the crowd. For the batsman it's often a relief when a fielder does make a minor error – half the time you are thinking, after playing a shot, 'That's worth runs,' but the field is too quick for you. This sort of pressure on the batsman is what Derek Randall and Paul Parker can apply so well. You can also imagine the tension building up on Randall, on the other side of the fence, when he is batting and being stymied by good fielding.

Randall is a memorable character. His 'lunacy' can drive people to distraction or keep them in stitches and the line between is often very fine. Stories about him are legion. One of the latest concerned an incident following his runs against India at Lord's, when he left the ground and turned right out of the Grace Gates. He then set off towards the Clarendon Court Hotel, Notts's usual residence in London, picked up key number 405 and took the lift. He had reached the door of the room when he remembered he should have had key 405 in his hand from the Westmoreland Hotel, where England stay, at the other end of St John's Wood Road.

Viv Richards

Ian Botham thinks Viv is a better batsman than Bradman and that to some people, especially Australians, is the ultimate heresy. To refute the argument that Bradman had to cope with far better bowling than Richards has faced, Ian points out, rightly, that Richards has scored his runs on far less reliable pitches, all around the world, in a half-dozen different types of cricket competitions and against restrictive field setting. It's a argument guaranteed to enliven any early-hours' conversation between cricketers. The one man I can believe would be utterly bored with it would be Viv himself, happy to leave the controversy in the good hands of Brother Botham.

No-one in cricket disputes that Viv has the ability to destroy any attack if and when he chooses. He has proved that he can annihilate bowlers even when the pressure has been intense and provide a stunning performance in the most dangerous situations when weaker spirits have foundered. Perhaps he needs a touch of the flame, a hint of crisis to bring out the best nowadays. A really big innings often seems to depend on incentives and driving forces – not so surprising when you think that West Indies, for all their talents, have depended on his keeping them on top now for something like eight years. Greenidge, Haynes, Kallicharran, Lloyd - they are all capable of big Test hundreds but the keystone to a West Indies' innings is invariably Viv. If he fails then it is such a psychological blow to them that they can look exceedingly vulnerable. If he succeeds then all the West Indians do is to unleash the fast bowlers – and another Test match is in the bag. That's why opposing captains, over the last few years, have concentrated on ways and means of dismissing Richards. Even when he's unfit he's dangerous: he got a century against Australia on one leg in 1979–80. During that triangular tour Viv had hip trouble but kept going; I can still remember a storming assault on Rodney Hogg in Melbourne – Hogg was bowling pretty quickly yet the more he bent his back the harder Viv hit him. It was sheer destruction.

Off the field Viv has a certain aristocratic air. People who don't know him, even players who have performed with and against him, are inclined to consider him off hand. 'He's too cool' is a fairly regular comment from players. There's a certain professional dislike for the obvious disdain Viv sometimes shows for the less gifted amongst us. I suspect that this is deliberate showmanship on Viv's part: he feels that he has to put it on a bit for the crowd and that playing well isn't always enough, especially for a West Indian crowd. They love the *macho*. None of this disdain shows in Viv's relationships off the field; in fact he tends to come across as a rather shy person and the press tell me he can appear insecure when dealing with them. It's something he will have to become accustomed to, because Clive Lloyd has been grooming him for the West Indies' captaincy for a long time. As a man and a cricketer his future seems gold-lined which is another reason, I suppose, why people look that much harder for the chinks.

Viv was lucky in the sense that his first two captains, and therefore major influences, were Brian Close at Somerset and Clive Lloyd with West Indies. Both have tried to instil in him that a stern century in the book is worth more than the most spectacular 65, and there are times when Viv clearly demonstrates that he has learned this lesson. And there are other occasions, to the delight of almost every spectator, when the bat is really put to the ball, as in 1977 when he hit a record number of sixes (26) in the John Player League. Viv always has style.

Viv Richards

No man in cricket dresses more smarly, has more shirts or listens to more music. Like Ian Botham he loves soccer and had a trial (centre half) with Bath City, but it came to nothing. His brother Mervyn is the national soccer coach in Antigua.

He won't find it easy to keep West Indies at the top, especially now that they, too, have come under the threat of South African encroachment. Of their quick bowlers it now seems certain that Colin Croft and Sylvester Clarke will not play for them again. Michael Holding and Joel Garner have both had their fitness problems, wear and tear, and Andy Roberts is approaching the veteran stage as quick bowler. Malcolm Marshall will probably appear as the senior fast bowler before very much longer, and the younger school was reduced by the defection of Franklyn Stephenson and Ezra Moseley to join their more senior colleagues in South Africa. Such is the depth of ability in the West Indies that they may be able to make up these losses far quicker than the world expects; but it will mean that Viv, unlike Clive, will not have another twenty or so Test-class players in reserve.

I can't believe that West Indies will suddenly turn to their many talented young spinners. Like Clive, Viv is a believer in quick bowling, despite being a more than useful off-spinner himself. He has sufficient control to bowl tightly enough to give away only a few runs, and then trades on his name! It's like facing Geoff Boycott's bowling, in that neither of them does really enough to get you out but the thought of making an error, and losing your wicket to either, can have a disturbing effect on your batting. If Viv were just another off-spinner you would play him as such. All he does really in the present set-up is to bowl a few overs to rest the quicks. If he does get a wicket, well, it's a bonus – it means that Michael and Andy and Joel have only the other nine to take. In fact, one of my haunting memories is being bowled by Viv in Barbados, having seen off the pacemen.

Viv's record is astonishing and the only threat to his continuing success seems to be fitness: he has had an eye complaint and a bad shoulder in the recent Indian series in the Caribbean. The strain of year-round cricket is telling on many of the world's top players with so much international cricket being played nowadays. For Somerset Viv has appeared tired and below his best though, as ever, fired by the big occasion and capable of extraordinary batting. He is already one of the great players – we shall have to wait to see what his eventual position in the game will be.

Andy Roberts

(LEEWARD ISLANDS, HAMPSHIRE,
LEICESTERSHIRE AND WEST INDIES)

Andy is the brains of the West Indian attack – and the best of it. They are all great bowlers, they've all learned a lot over the past seven years but Andy, the oldest and the shrewdest, tops them all. Colin Croft can be more hostile, Michael Holding is faster, Joel Garner is all awkward angles and sudden bounce, while Malcolm Marshall is high-speed deception, the ball skidding on to you faster than you expect.

Andy thinks you out, He's quieter even than Michael, almost taciturn, and had the reputation while he was with Hampshire of being moody. Arriving in England from Antigua as a stranger I can imagine he would be socially ill at ease. Born of a large fishing family, he's a strict non-drinker and I get the impression that he's seen what can come from over indulgence. A glass of orange juice, or a coke, is as far as he will go, which obviously does no harm to his fitness. Although his bones do not take too happily to English temperatures he knows exactly what he needs to do as regards training, stretching and preparing to be as right as possible for his next cricketing commitments. One desperate failure to bend far enough in the field led to my giving him the tag of 'Sideboard' – they don't move too easily, either! Last winter he went home to Antigua and settled for fishing and swimming for three months before adding a schedule of running and stamina work prior to the start of the Shell Shield competition. This approach and his natural ability have extended his life as a top-class fast bowler despite having been apparently eased out of the West Indies' side a couple of times, only to force his way back and reclaim the new ball.

Andy has been very good for Leicestershire, helping Les Taylor to give us a genuine strike force and setting a fine example to younger bowlers such as Gordon Parsons and Jon Agnew. Gordon took the mickey out of Andy for much of the summer but it was Andy who had the last laugh when, one day, he aptly referred to Gordon as 'Bullhead', a nickname that quickly stuck. Andy's humour is dry, cutting and rare but when he does deliver a line it's a good one, always accompanied by one of those great, wide West Indian grins. We don't see much of him after a match and on away games he likes to eat early and well, then disappear to bed. Perhaps more of us would benefit from a similar discipline!

One summer's day in Canterbury three car-loads set off for a supper of fish and chips, despite Andy's protests that he needed something more substantial. And what happened? Andy finished his portion first and dived back in for a second helping – a considerable tribute to Canterbury fish and chips. His contribution to a book of recipes which Brian Davison's wife assembled for Brian's benefit year also amused us: Andy's meal-portions of pumpkin soup and fried chicken would have fed at least eight. I hope I haven't given the impression that Leicestershire's diet centres upon cod and fried chicken. We gourmets have to indulge ourselves sometimes!

Andy's enthusiasm for continuous cricket is not what it once might have been. His ambition is to be involved in a big one-day final for the county, having never achieved that with Hampshire. His bowling certainly gave us a great chance of sneaking the championship in 1982. Andy shattered Glamorgan, leaving us only two points behind Middlesex with two games each to play. It wasn't Andy's fault that we lost our way after that.

One of his greatest assets is that he always talks a lot of good cricket sense and on those occasions when we've roomed together and he's been awake when I've got in, we have had

some long and worthwhile discussions on the game. He's certainly not wasted his experience in international cricket and his knowledge could be of benefit to anyone prepared to take the time to talk to him. Andy is 32 this year, so how much longer he will stay at Leicester is unknown. His importance to us will be as much to assist our own hopefuls as to destroy opposition batting. Andy will also be nurturing Antigua's latest prospect, George Ferris, who is joining Leicestershire. Although I shan't be too pleased if young George becomes yet another West Indian Test cricketer developed in England, I do hope his talents will be exploited fully by Leicestershire, and we can't have it both ways, after all. For the present Grace Road hopes to see many more of those sudden fiery spells from Andy.

Bob Taylor

(DERBYSHIRE AND ENGLAND)

As Chris Martin-Jenkins points out in his *Who's Who of Test Cricket* – 'Of all the good and bad repercussions of the Packer Revolution the happiest was that this perfect craftsman and ideal sportsman suddenly acquired a status which his exceptional ability warranted.'

I would never have liked to try and compare Bob Taylor and Alan Knott in terms of ability and everyone agreed that it was a shame, but inevitable, that Bob had to play deputy to Knott for 10 years. When Alan virtually withdrew himself from Test cricket there was a general feeling that at last justice could be done to Bob.

Once established Bob set off on a record-breaking spree that shows no signs of stopping or even slowing down. His last was J. T. Murray's world record of first-class victims (1,527) which Bob was due to overtake in our opening match of last winter's tour of Australia, against Queensland in Brisbane. The team were all wound up for the big moment, but three times fairly confident appeals for catches behind were all turned down, with all the England side ready to rush in to give him a 'Well done, Bob' and some heartfelt congratulations. In the end, after those three false starts, we had to wait until the second innings and then, ironically, for Bob to establish his new world's best with a stumping! The exceptionally hospitable Queensland Association, and Cricketers' Club, had no intention of allowing any history made at the Gabba to pass unnoticed and duly claimed the ball to have it mounted and presented to Bob. It would be nice to think that someone back home was also thinking of some way of recognizing a tremendous achievement by a genius of a wicketkeeper.

Not all geniuses can be regarded as nice guys but Bob is at the top as a professional and a human being; there is little doubt that if the world's cricketers were to vote on the player all small boys should try to emulate then R. W. Taylor would win by a landslide. Even in his forties he's still right at the top as a keeper and still insists – and who's to argue? – that he's working on his batting. He is as fitness-conscious as anyone, training more regularly than most to help himself through a day's keeping, the strain of which not many spectators appreciate. It is a tribute to this effort that it is only now that age has started to catch up. For the first time, on the last Australian tour, I heard Bob admit to be slightly tired and stiff after a day in the field.

His appetite for work and his wonderful attitude to the job make him a tremendous influence for good in the dressing-rooms while his experience – he's been playing first-class cricket for twenty-three years – provides his captain with vast cricket knowledge. His attitude was summed up by another incident a little later last winter when England's reserve, Ian Gould, was injured during a match against New South Wales. Rick McCosker graciously gave permission for Bob to take over the gloves, although he was supposed to be having one of his rare matches off. It's always a strange feeling appearing in a game in which technically you are not supposed to be involved. Bob, however, settled in as quietly and effectively as ever and did the job for the rest of the day, happy to be practising his art. Happily, we also won the game.

Bob is far more than just the England wicketkeeper. While he gives his own job total concentration he also has time to keep everyone going with a word to the bowlers, advice if requested to the captain, and always an eye on his fielders, making sure they are on their toes. Bob resigned the Derbyshire captaincy because he felt it was affecting his wicketkeeping, although he

seemed to be the only man who had noticed. When he does eventually leave the England dressing-room his tactical insight will be only one of very many virtues that will be missed. When that time comes and the selectors do have to make a decision on a replacement for their old-time, old-style, all-star top professional, it will be a very difficult one.

Paul Downton (Middlesex) should still be in the frame; Ian Gould has many of the assets of David Bairstow and, like David, may find he'll play in more one-day internationals than Tests; Jack Richards and Bruce French are possibles. None of them yet stands out in the same way as Bob and whoever assumes his mantle will have a long tradition of high-class keeping to maintain. Meanwhile we should all enjoy Bob while he's still got the job. Let's admire that certain honesty that seems to envelop everything he does, let's still smile or applaud when he pulls off one of those amazing legside catches or when he is charming the socks off some Caribbean Marxist diplomat at the next High Commission party. And let's not overlook another facet of the amazing RWT. He also happens to be a top tourist who, along with Bernard Thomas, always knows where to go, how to get there, and what to buy.

Perhaps it was this love of touring, and his fierce loyalty to the game, that kept him going through those long depressing years in Knott's shadow. It cannot have been pleasant to be asked, as he was in New Zealand several years ago, by a well-intentioned and polite woman after spotting his tour blazer: 'And who might you be?' Bob was wearing one of those little plastic cards bearing his name!

While Knott was admitting, privately, that he thought Bob the better 'keeper it was only in cricket's inner circle that Bob's status was fully recognized until, that is, Mr Packer appeared.

Bob was spotted by Cliff Gladwin while playing for a North Staffordshire League club, Bignall End, and he still lives on the edge of the Potteries. He gives Stoke City almost as much devotion as Derbyshire and named his house 'Hambledon', the source of a much treasured story in the county dressing-room.

Asked where Bob lived, a colleague replied: 'I can tell you where it is but don't ask me the address. It's a house with a funny name.'

Another Derbyshire legend is of Alan Ward checking with the batsman as to whether Bob had actually dropped a catch! The fast bowler didn't believe it until the batsman admitted a nick. Taylor-watchers, who congregate in large numbers in the Peak, tell you the give-away is the slight droop of the head for a moment before the next delivery. He once told Michael Carey: 'If I'm keeping badly it's usually because of one of three reasons: lack of concentration, standing up too soon, or snatching at the ball. The longer you stay down, even for a thousandth of a second, may mean the difference between the ball glancing off your fingertips or sticking in the middle of your glove. I am a professional, others rely on me and as far as I am concerned it is a crime to let them down.'

Bob Willis

Bob Willis is not the easiest man to know immediately. In my first Test alongside him, against Pakistan, he was always on a different wavelength from me, on and off the field; the difference between senior and junior player seemed quite apparent. It wasn't until I had toured with him that I got to know him better, and he me, realizing that our sense of humour was very alike. In fact, he was responsible for my initial England nickname. I also appreciate what a warm and sympathetic character lies below that fierce, sometimes aggressive regard for standards. Once you have convinced him that you do care very much for the way the game is played, on and off the field, that you can do your job up to his measurements, you have his respect and friendship. On that score I think I have now overcome his initial criticism of me for a lack of professionalism and application.

Curiously, I have rarely faced Bob Willis in county cricket, a measure of the demands made by international fixtures in the last decade. I played against Ian Botham only twice in three seasons and on the second occasion, in 1980, he wasn't bowling! I make this point to put into context the often-heard criticism that Bob is a different bowler for Warwickshire. Most of the years Bob has bowled at Edgbaston it has been a slow, flat track that would have broken the heart of anyone trying to bowl fast. The first-hand evidence I can offer is that of watching Bob bowl countless overs for England and on those occasions, almost without exception, his performance would have to be described as superb.

He will always be very tense on the field. When he's trying hard and the whole team are trying hard with him he cannot bear to see the initiative slip away. In one of his overs he will come tearing in, ball after ball, expending every ounce of effort and if he doesn't get a breakthrough, or a chance is missed, he will stalk away with that tight expression on his face, eyes blazing. People tend to be put off by that kind of intensity and it is necessary to get to know him to appreciate him. For instance, Mike Brearley was reported to have said in the *Sun* newspaper, that Bob is 'nothing but a psyched-up fast bowler'. Whatever Mike said I'm sure he didn't say it quite like that, because he knows that while Bob may tear in like a tornado he can also be objective enough to control a side throughout a five-day Test match.

Bob has the presence of a captain. You look up to him in lots of senses – tall, bright-eyed, that great mop of hair, a very imposing presence. He won a lot of respect with most of the England regulars when he was vice-captain under Brearley, Botham and Fletcher, for almost four years – always the hard senior professional, making sure that whatever the captain wanted was done. Those present haven't forgotten that morning in Colombo in 1981 when, briefly, it seemed just possible that England could lose in the very first Test match played by Sri Lanka. Before we went out Bob really laid into us: 'After four months out here I don't want to go home losing to this lot so let's go out there and play as an England team should play. I'll tell you this – if we do lose to Sri Lanka then you won't want to go home!' We went out, John Emburey particularly bowled very well, and we were able to fly home with some self-respect.

I think Bob also learned something from the way the change of captaincy was made. Keith Fletcher was a very skilful captain, in my opinion, subtle in his tactics and methods of exerting pressure, and he might have had a very successful career as England's captain but for that one defeat in Bombay.

We lost to India on that occasion by over-confidence. After arriving in India the team had played well, all the batsmen had runs, the bowlers were fit and felt in form and on the previous occasion we had played at the Wankhede Stadium, in the Jubilee Test, neither the pitch nor the Indian team had given us many difficulties. This time, under Fletcher, faced with much better bowling, a pitch that was breaking up and contentious umpiring decisions, we were in the mire before we realized what was happening. Going one down, Fletcher was never able to level the series on slow flat pitches where India were quite happy not to lose.

I think most of the players still expected Fletcher to carry on as captain and it must have hit him very hard to lose the job. Certainly the change did no harm in terms of results: Bob led us to two series victories, the second against the strong Pakistan team a notable triumph, and we also cleaned up in the Prudential Cup matches against both sides.

Bob's major examination came in Australia, where I think he got most things right. He took a traditional stance on the way players should behave on and off the field, insisting on certain standards of conduct, dress and match preparation. His own experience has taught him just how much is needed in terms of work, exercise and diet on tour to maintain mobility and fitness. He was stern enough, firm enough and, as I have said, he always had Botham's respect, no matter what you may have read.

The fact that Bob Willis has come through so many injuries and setbacks to remain England's fast bowler until well into his thirties gives him an authority on the subject and treatment of fast bowlers that few will challenge, even among the selectors. He is listened to with great respect. For instance, while I know Bob appreciated Graham Dilley's many assets, as a captain I guess he is unsure just how much Graham really wants to bowl fast and take wickets. In Bob's mind there is the question: is Graham hard enough for the job or confident enough to become hard?

Willis took a lot of criticism in England for his treatment of Norman Cowans, yet much of that criticism came from people who cannot have appreciated how much of an apprentice Norman was on his first tour. Norman came out with us not only learning to be a fast bowler, hard enough in itself, but also learning to be a cricketer. We played Norman at Perth in his first Test match, following an impressive performance against Western Australia in the previous match. A combination of nerves, inexperience and a belligerent Chappell, apparently bent on destroying the young man's confidence, resulted in a disappointing performance in which Norman never reached full pace and, at one stage, was pulled by Chappell three times to the boundary in one over. More than once on the tour we found it hard to get Norman going. At Sydney against New South Wales he bowled very fast one evening, incensed at being run out, but next morning failed to achieve anything like the same fire. In Tasmania a similar pattern emerged, so one could be forgiven for being hesitant about putting Norman in to bowl, or for being apprehensive about what might happen in the context of a Test match. It's true that there were several occasions when Norman wasn't at his best on tour, when he had niggling aches or sprains to knees and ankles. These, in turn, raised more questions: was he prone to niggling injuries? Could he come through them?

Bob had to lay down the law, to point out that bowling on Australian turf, in Australian light and heat, takes a toll of anybody. Fast bowling anywhere, but especially in Australia, is an examination of strength, resilience and concentration. If you go down with little bumps or bruises or pains you won't get very far. A captain has to know that his fast bowlers are capable of bowling fast at least three times a day. All these things were in Bob's mind when he considered calling up Norman for another spell and, indeed, when the question of Norman's selection for the Test side itself came up. Any suggestions that Cowans was selected over the captain's head are nonsense; the captain always has the last word and it was at the captain's

Bob Willis

insistence that Norman played in Brisbane. The charge that Bob Willis had a down on Norman Cowans came in that Second Test at Brisbane, where the Australian first innings, under great pressure, was rallied by Kepler Wessels and a firstly nervous and then increasingly confident Bruce Yardley. In that entire innings Cowans bowled only six overs. It was this I think which raised the suspicion that Willis didn't want him in the side.

There was no other reason than that it was our strategy in keeping it tight. Norman could have cost us twenty or twenty-four runs very quickly, opening the way for Australia. In a sense this did happen: Brisbane was a Test match we could and should have won against an Australian team that was, at that time, rocky and vulnerable after the draw in Perth and the loss, through injury, of Dennis Lillee and Terry Alderman. Bob was rightly upset by the Brisbane defeat. He was annoyed by the fact that he had to finish off their first innings by himself – as he did, superbly – and angry that his batsmen had let him down, as he had every right to be. England should never have been bowled out for 290. It's not as if the batsmen who played were out of form or out of runs, and even if Graeme Fowler had to be thrown in at the deep end there were six other batsmen at least one of whom should have had a century. If two batsmen had scored centuries we couldn't have lost that match (even another 50 runs would probably have won it) and the whole tempo of the series would have been changed. For obvious reasons I am as much aware as anyone of what went wrong in Brisbane, and for the captain's deep disappointments.

Bob's reaction was typical of the man. He decided that Norman had to be entirely physically fit before turning him into a strike bowler, not just fit to be a Test fast bowler. Bob's own fitness training is immaculate and he laid down a similar schedule for Norman between the Brisbane and Adelaide Tests, calling in Gladstone Small, who was playing grade cricket in Melbourne, to help. Three-mile runs were programmed to build up Norman's stamina, the object being to make him as fit and fresh in his second and third six-over spells as he was in his first. Thus we were able to reintroduce Norman for the Fourth Test in Melbourne.

He bowled well enough in the first innings for everyone to be satisfied with the effort, removing Dyson and Chappell, the latter hooking, with successive balls. The second innings was his moment of glory on the tour, taking 6 for 69; although he was helped by the pitch, which gave an erratic bounce, we managed to awake a fire in him and to keep the blaze going, telling him, repeatedly, 'You're not tired, you're not tired,' when he was almost out on his feet. In that one spell, however, Norman should have boosted his confidence enormously and have learned more about the real demands of fast bowling. The effort has to be applied consistently and let us hope it will not be too long before he repeats that performance.

Working and living with Bob Willis for four months will have done Norman no harm, because Bob is an amazing example to us all. To go through an Australian tour as well as he did, at his age, with all the wear and tear and strain on his body, is a tribute to his own character and to the efficiency of his training. It is probably the only Australian tour Bob has survived unscathed! As a quick bowler you do pretty well to go through an English summer without a breakdown. Then to go out to Australia, where there's no give in the ground, where you are bowling day after day in the heat and the glare and where there's very little time between fixtures in the television age – to succeed in that you need to be a superman. A fast bowler's feet are soon blistered and stay blistered. The big toe takes such a pounding that it has become a common sight in the England dressing-room to see Bernard Thomas, the physiotherapist, working on the captain's feet. To draw the blood Bernard has to sink a heated needle through the big toe-nail. It's nasty and it's painful, but Bob Willis has gone through it a thousand times and accepts it as the price that has to be paid to be a Test bowler.

There were more than physical problems. The decision to

send Australia in at Adelaide raised a storm that will rumble on for a long time, but Bob had full backing from the five selectors for what seemed to be perfectly logical at the time. He had seen the wicket looking very wet the day before and couldn't believe that there wouldn't be a residue of moisture under the pitch for at least the first morning. Knowing Adelaide's reputation for providing the flattest batting wickets in Australia, it seemed to make further sense to reserve the better batting conditions for our first innings rather than expose the England batsmen to Lawson, Thomson and the returning Rodney Hogg, on his home wicket, in what could be the most dangerous and crucial session of the match. We all know what happened. This pitch turned out to be the flattest we've ever known, right from the start, and it didn't take long before second slip (Botham) called to gully (Gower): 'I think we might have got this wrong.'

Bob's judgements were conditioned by the Brisbane Test, which we had expected to win but had batted badly against an erratic bounce. The Australians meanwhile were, as Bob put it, 'getting it right by accident'. Having lost Lillee and Alderman through injury, they had to recall the apparently faded Thomson and promote Rackemann for Brisbane. Thomson proved there that he could still bowl quickly, even if he overdid the short-pitched stuff. He wasn't as accurate as Hogg or Lawson but he did bowl with fire and was fast enough and short enough to upset our batsmen and force them into awkward positions, although the Australians admitted privately he could no longer make it 'spit' or lift as in his heyday when, apparently, he didn't have to drop it short to make it fly. Australia then lost Rackemann, injured, in Brisbane and consequently won the series with Lawson, Thomson and Hogg, three bowlers more capable of buffeting our batsmen, who are more accustomed to dealing with the problems of line and length, as would have been set by Lillee and Alderman, than a persistent attack short of a length.

Greg Chappell's tactics at Adelaide were to use his three quick men in short bursts from one end and seek to contain us by Yardley's slow medium off-breaks at the other. After Adelaide we did our best to upset this plan by making a more conscious attempt to attack Yardley – Chris Tavaré, especially, driving him to all parts. That made Greg think again, occasionally having to bowl himself, which gave us a little respite. At the end of that first morning in Adelaide we had to try to keep things tight. We had to try to make sure they didn't get away, even though Chappell was in flight. We succeeded to some extent: we did come back from 264 for 2 to Australia 438 all out, not a bad effort. Bob couldn't be blamed for the batting, about which he was very disappointed. Where we fell apart was in losing eight wickets for 76 runs in the first innings, after reaching 140 for two, needing 239 to avoid a follow on and then, even worse, losing the last six wickets of the second innings for 65 after climbing to 236 for 4. Avoiding the follow-on was crucial to that match; once we had failed to do that all Bob could do was reprove and exhort, then leave it to the batsmen to try to save us.

At Melbourne, after four days of very tense cricket, the worst was still to come. With the game apparently won, as last man Jeff Thomson came to the crease with Australia still needing 74 runs to win, we embarked on a strategy of trying to contain his partner Allan Border with deep spread fields while attacking Thomson at the other end. As the score edged nearer the target it became increasingly easy for people to suggest that in not pressuring Border we were in error, especially when one edge slid away through the vacant second slip position. The tension was almost unbearable on that final morning as the remaining 37 runs required dwindled to four when, at last, our tactics worked and an immensely satisfying victory was completed. Certainly the margin was too close for any sort of comfort but the odds always were that our strategy would succeed long before it did. One must give credit to Border for manipulating affairs so well in a situation that seemed to bring out the best in him. Extra credit, also, to Norman Cowans, for his efforts to get us into that winning position.

So Bob's task at Sydney was to try to inspire us to repeat the victory, against history and the odds. He almost set us off perfectly by running out Dyson without a run on the board, only for the decision to go against us. That, and Kim Hughes's century virtually settled the match and the series, a sad way to finish. Throughout the Test series and the subsequent one-day competitions, which can be conservatively described as an up and down affair, Bob maintained his spirit, humour and dignity, always facing the press and television when required, whatever disasters had befallen us. The long tour undoubtedly took its toll of his mental reserves, as it did for most of us, and it's a shame that the tour results will detract from what has been an immensely impressive career for Bob Willis, whose heart, when playing for England, has been bigger than anyone's.

David Gower

by Derek Hodgson

Searching mind and memory for the words to describe the style of the player and the man, I started thinking that it was a shame that neither of those masters of the cricketing vignette, Cardus and Robertson-Glasgow, are alive to contribute their impressions of David Gower, one no doubt in oils, one in charcoal.

David's career has flowered a little late, even for John Arlott, although the Mage of Alderney could yet commit himself to a long piece while lifting an occasional glass in David's honour. Then the clue surfaced: Frank Woolley.

It was Cardus, I remembered, who had written so lyrically of Woolley – like Gower, a tall willowy left-hander from Kent. Cardus, too, had run a little short of words and, in casting around for a loan, had found a phrase so evocative it has stayed in my mind for more than thirty years. Sir Neville, bless him, never had the slightest scruples about borrowing from other sources in the rare event of drying up: he would no doubt argue that there is nothing dishonourable in derivative writing.

Cardus didn't let me down. In the Rupert Hart-Davis (1949) edition of '*Days in the Sun*' there is one chapter entitled 'Woolley: An Appreciation' which is delightful enough in its way: 'One thinks of him as a butterfly in a city street on a summer's day.' Yet a better starting point is the essay 'Frank Woolley' in the companion volume *Good Days*. This comes from what Cardus would refer to later as his 'salad green' period, before the later years of fame and fortune. If there is an innocence about his earlier cricket writings there is also the freshness that stems from youth and idealism. The lines that have stuck in my mind since 1950 turned out to be a quotation that Cardus used to illustrate Woolley's stroke-making:

> Lovely are the curves of the white owl sweeping,
> Wavy in the dusk lit by one large star.

To which Cardus adds, as if more than a little embarrassed: 'I admit, O reader, that an innings by Woolley has nothing to do with owls and dusk and starlight. I am trying to describe an experience of the fancy: I am talking of cadences, of dying falls common to all the beauty of the world.' The poetry is by the Victorian novelist, George Meredith, who, if little read nowadays, may have been a powerful influence on the young Cardus. He did imbibe some heady brews in his young Manchester days: MacLaren, Spooner and Jessop at Old Trafford, the Hallé playing Mahler at the Free Trade Hall and Mr Meredith inflaming his senses with lovely curves.

Yes, all this is relevant to David Gower. I make no apologies. We have now come full circle. To see Gower driving or cutting in a scented English dusk at Worcester, in a Jamaican sunset below the Blue Mountains, perhaps on a dusty red-gold evening in Delhi, is to see the curves of the white owl. There is no sinuous West Indian, upright Australian or striding Pakistani who can match Gower today for sheer beauty of stroke. When God smiles on him he puts bat to ball and no more than a fleeting kiss propels it to the fence with the velocity of a cannon ball. The elegance of the movement, the timing of the contact, would delight a courtier of the Sun King or make a fencing master jealous.

He also has his all-too-human days. He was twenty-six last April and up to a year ago he was regularly criticised for what were interpreted as 'his attitudes'. 'You can't tell him anything' complained one of cricket's elder statesmen shaking his head sadly, in Sydney, three years ago. 'He just smiles and carries on.' He was, wrote colleagues, 'lacking in application, a dreamer, irresponsible'. His dismissals were analysed, his alleged weaknesses probed in print and on camera. He did his stint in the nets and no more, openly questioning the value of long practice on poor surfaces, a sharp contrast to the methods of some senior colleagues.

Much of this fire flew in through the generation gap. He didn't act or talk or play like the majority of the cricketers of twenty-five years ago, so this to them was one good reason why he failed occasionally. Appearing not to absorb advice isn't the same as rejecting it. What works for Geoff Boycott doesn't necessarily work for Derek Randall – or for David Gower. While the barbs were flying he lost his temper only once to my knowledge; that amounts to a clean sheet in virtually six years of concentrated attention from the media. Journalists who have worked with him on newspaper articles credit him with punctuality, availability, ideas and considerable good humour under stress. The grizzled society of ghostwriters, inured to chiselling words out of less reliable Big Names, long ago awarded the Good Conduct Magnum to D. I. Gower.

Home environment steered him towards a career of learning and responsibility. His father was in the Colonial Service, which meant that the young David spent his first six years in the then Tanganyika before returning to his native county of Kent and Marlborough House prep school in Hawkhurst. In 1965 David's father became registrar of Loughborough College, the son attending school in Quorn before attending King's, Canterbury where, in the last of his three seasons in the first XI, he made two centuries. A keen Leicestershire supporter, noting his promise, sent his name to Grace Road. With eight O-levels and three A-levels, he failed to win a place at Oxford but he was admitted to University College, London, reading law and playing second team and under-twenty-five matches for Leicestershire, they having gained Kent's permission ('to our astonishment and delight' records secretary manager Mike Turner) to register him.

He had toured West Indies and South Africa with the

English Schools' XI but he wasn't committed at that stage to a cricketing career, although he already knew that he was bored with his university subject. The influence of hardened Yorkshire professionals in exile at Grace Road, Ray Illingworth and Jack Birkenshaw, and his introduction to the first team in 1975, finally persuaded him to seek his living from the game. By 1978 he was playing Test cricket, becoming at twenty-one the youngest English batsman since Peter May to make a Test century.

Henry Blofeld still remembers that first Test innings: 'On Friday, June 2, shortly after lunch, Gower came out of the pavilion at Edgbaston to play his first Test innings with the score at 101 for 2. Brearley had been run out and Gower had to wait for his first ball. These were two or three minutes which would have created butterflies in the hardest of stomachs.

'Gower has that thoroughbred walk which marks him as an athlete of distinction before the pavilion gate is ten yards behind him. He took guard, outwardly relaxed, looked round the field before settling into that tidy, classical left-handed stance. Liaquat Ali, fast medium left arm over the wicket, began his slanting run from the Press Box End.

Just before Ali reached the crease Gower gave two modest taps of the bat against his left toe. The ball came down, it was short, pitching maybe on the line of the middle stump and with the angle of delivery going across Gower to the legside.

'He saw the ball early with precise, unfussy footwork, moved outside the line and hooked. The bat made that satisfying resonant sound as it struck the ball and long leg could only jog round to his right to retrieve it after it had crashed into the fencing in front of the Rae Bank Stand.

'It was the most conclusive and emphatic entry into Test cricket that any batsman can ever have made. That stroke and the preamble leading up to it, summed up admirably the temperament and the approach of David Gower, who is still only twenty-one, and yet already a batsman anyone in the world would be glad to come and watch.'

Epilogue: David Gower, by Derek Hodgson

That memorable first ball was recalled a little differently by the batsman, talking to Michael Carey: 'As I walked out I was thinking "Hang on, this is a Test match. You must get your feet moving. You mustn't freeze out there". So I hooked the first ball for four and then thought "Heavens, what have I done? It could have gone anywhere. Suppose I had been caught?" Surprisingly, you may think, I do not regard that as an ideal way to start an innings. I much prefer to begin slowly. That way I think I'm likely to have more runs.'

It was after his second Australian tour, 1979–80, that the critics took aim at Gower. He admits he did not have a successful time: 98 in the second innings at Sydney was his best and he totalled 54 runs in another five innings. Robin Marlar detected a weakness shared with Woolley: 'While Gower has the priceless asset of swinging the bat at the ball – a gift the cricketing gods lavished on Woolley, Neil Harvey, Graeme Pollock and Gary Sobers – he also has that degree of anatomical stiffness which can make footwork restricted and batting difficult. To many who saw him, criticism of Woolley is sacrilege. Yet his Test record is poor. In his mature years he walked as erect and stiff as a guardsman; was this the reason, lack of correct movement of his feet when confronted by the world's best bowling, which made Woolley fallible?'

The *Sunday Times* cricket correspondent concluded (in 1980): 'He has it in him to be a left-handed version of Jack Hobbs. The next three years will show us whether he is to go into history as a talented batsman or a great one.' Since then, apart from two occasions when the selectors chose to leave him out, David has been an England fixture, playing in all forty-four Tests. He needs another hundred runs to reach his 3,000, is averaging 46 and although he has only five Test centuries he has passed 50 in Tests fifteen times.

Those figures are just the nuts and bolts. More pertinent facts involve the eight hours he batted against a Young West Indies' XI to score 187 in Trinidad on the opening match of the tour in January 1981, a derisive salute to those who said he couldn't concentrate. There was the brilliant 200 against India at Edgbaston in 1979, the grit-and-guts century, with a rock-like Boycott to guide him, against Australia at Perth in 1978 and then, most of all, the succession of defiant yet commanding innings against Australia in 1982–3, the tour 'lit by one large star'. Finally, as if to prove himself the very model of a modern major batsman, he tore into New Zealand in the one-day matches, leaving the impression, to depressed Englishmen at home, of lightning flashes in a black sky.

David Gower now lives in a spacious, handsome post-war house a mile from Grace Road. The sitting-room overflows with books and records – his musical tastes range from Vivaldi to Dire Straits – and if time allows, he finishes the *Daily Telegraph* crossword most days. Despite five England tours he enjoys holiday travelling: to Venice on the Orient Express, to Switzerland and the mountains, to Burgundy villages. He enjoys good food and wine, conversation and Monty Python, powerful cars and blue seas.

So far David Gower hasn't given much thought to his future after playing, but as he enjoys cricket and cricket people so much I believe he is likely to want to keep a place in the sun. Television, radio or a newspaper will find that place for him. He enjoys communication and could therefore become a good communicator. This assessment of his heroes and contemporaries, made not even in mid-career, has been a good exercise in assessments and judgement, both the source and the subjects offering some historical value to cricket's library. I am certainly looking forward to reading a sequel, a second volume to be published in, say, 1993.

Manchester-Sydney-Brisbane-Melbourne-Adelaide-Leicester

SEPTEMBER 1982 TO MARCH 1983

ACKNOWLEDGEMENTS

To:
Wisden Cricketers' Almanac
Wisden Cricket Monthly
Cricketer International
Who's Who of Test Cricketers by Christopher Martin-Jenkins
    (Orbis)
The Cricketers' Who's Who ed. Iain Sproat
Living for Cricket by Clive Lloyd with Tony Crozier (Stanley
    Paul)
From Bradman to Boycott by Ted Dexter (Queen Anne Press)

And to Vicki Stewart, whose sandwiches could sustain an innings by Gavaskar; and Connie Whitworth, whose dexterity is equalled only by Qadir.